THE POET'S SELF
AND THE POEM

ERICH HELLER

The Poet's Self
and the Poem

ESSAYS ON GOETHE,
NIETZSCHE, RILKE AND
THOMAS MANN

UNIVERSITY OF LONDON
THE ATHLONE PRESS
1976

Published by
THE ATHLONE PRESS
UNIVERSITY OF LONDON
at 4 *Gower Street London* WC1

Distributed by Tiptree Book Services Ltd
Tiptree, Essex

U.S.A. and Canada
Humanities Press Inc
New Jersey

© *Erich Heller* 1976

ISBN 0 485 11164 0

Printed in Great Britain by
WESTERN PRINTING SERVICES
BRISTOL

In Memoriam
HANNAH ARENDT

PREFACE

What follows is the text—a little longer than the spoken version—of the four Lord Northcliffe Lectures that I had the privilege to give at University College London in the spring of 1975. I am most grateful to University College and its Provost, Lord Annan, for appointing me to this lectureship (and for the generous hospitality that went with it) as well as to the Athlone Press of the University of London for making the lectures available in print. When a few weeks after my stay in London I visited Israel, I was asked to repeat them at the Van Leer Foundation in Jerusalem. The introductory remarks I made there are, I believe, not unsuitable to preface this volume.

'It is perhaps still a little unusual for a visitor to this city to lecture on subjects entirely derived from the history of German literature and thought. Or would it be wiser to say: subjects that *seem* to be specifically German? This is not an apology but a pointer to what I believe to be the much wider, the supranational significance of the problems I am about to discuss: the varied and intriguing relationships between life as everyone knows it in his day-to-day routine and a less customary activity of human minds: the making of poems. "Poem" is the term I have used in the collective title of these lectures although what I mean by it is certainly not confined to its usual English meaning, that is, a specimen of the genre "poetry". No, I mean any configuration of words such as have been written by Nietzsche or Thomas Mann, verbal compositions that, even without their aspiring to verse or rhyme, bear witness to the poetic faculty of man. In fact the German usage of *"Dichtung"* comes close enough to my meaning. I am sure we would lose sight of this at our peril—even in times when and places of the world where "peril" suggests something more urgent, more menacing, and more painful than the word normally conveys. But would we in our perilous lives have to defend anything worth defending if we forsook the mind of poetry—poetry, once more, to be understood as comprehensively as possible: as the outcome of the desire, indeed the need, to give form, communicable form, to the nature of the soul, its pleasures, sorrows, and aspirations? And asking this question, we cease to speak "merely" German.'

My thanks are due to Putnam and Co. Inc. for permission to reprint in this volume as 'Nietzsche in the Waste Land' a chapter first included in the fourth edition (1974) of *The Disinherited Mind*, and to Random House Inc. for allowing me to draw on material from my Introduction to their edition of *Death in Venice*, translated by Kenneth Burke (1970), in the chapter 'Thomas Mann in Venice'.

Northwestern University   E. H.
Evanston, Illinois
Autumn 1975

CONTENTS

I

Goethe in Marienbad

It was in 1823 that Johann Peter Eckermann took up his celebrated role as Goethe's secretary and partner in conversation: his *Conversations with Goethe* was later listed by Nietzsche among the four best German works in prose. On 10 November of that year Goethe showed Eckermann his poem 'The Pariah', asked him to read it and tell him what he thought about it. Eckermann, rather evasively, said that his imagination had a hard time in 'endowing it with life'. In other words: he did not understand it. Goethe was not surprised. Its treatment, he said, is very condensed and one has to live with it for quite a while in order to make it one's own: 'After all, I myself have carried it about in my mind for forty years and so it had plenty of time to cleanse itself of everything superfluous.' It will, Eckermann replied rather timidly, impress its readers. Yet should one not perhaps heighten its effect by prefacing it with an explanation? Such a procedure has often proved useful in the case of paintings representing unusual subjects. But Goethe would have none of this. With paintings it is a different matter, he answered. But because a poem, like its explanation, is made of words, these two kinds of words are bound to get into each other's way.—Well, yes, Eckermann saw the problem, but none the less asked himself whether it would be really impossible, 'to help a poem to be understood without in the slightest harming its delicate inner life?'

This, then, may serve as the motto of these explorations. Their theme is not only Goethe's 'Elegy', known as the Marienbad Elegy, the longest and, in the judgement of many,

the greatest of Goethe's love poems, but also, in a sense, the
fifty years that Goethe had to live through in order to write it.
How is this? Is the 'Elegy' not the result of a *'Liebschaft'*, a love
entanglement, as Goethe himself called his relationship to
Ulrike von Levetzow four years later,[1] a *'Liebschaft'* that inter-
mittently lasted three summers, having gently begun in 1821
when Goethe was seventy-two and Ulrike von Levetzow
seventeen. She was the daughter of Amalie von Levetzow, an
old acquaintance of Goethe's, whose name appears in his diary
as early as July 1806 with the mysterious but strangely prophetic
addendum 'Pandora'. This *'Liebschaft'*, then, ended abruptly in
1823 with a private agony, a lyrical scandal, and that social
embarrassment the memory of which was still alive when
Thomas Mann, in 1911, conceived the plan for a novella
'Goethe in Marienbad' and wrote *Death in Venice* instead.

The 'Elegy' is rightly called after Marienbad, the youngest,
most attractive, and at that time most fashionable of the Bohemian watering-places. We know for certain that the poem
came into being at the beginning of September 1823 in the
travelling coach that took Goethe back to Weimar from the
Bohemian woods.[2] Goethe himself called it 'the product of a
very impassioned state'. He wrote it 'from relay to relay', and
this is why, as he explained only two months later to Eckermann, it possesses 'a certain spontaneity' and is 'of a piece'.[3] Yet
it does not merely express the impassioned state of this traveller
at this particular time, but a state of soul which Goethe had
occasion to contemplate for at least fifty years: it repeated itself
time and time again ever since he wrote *The Sufferings of Young
Werther*, the book whose fiftieth birthday was to be celebrated
in the following year—1824—with a jubilee edition. The
Leipzig publisher Weygand enquired whether Goethe would
not write an introduction. He would not know what to say or

how to freshen his memory, Goethe replied.[4] Indeed, how should he 'remember' what had just been immediate presence? When Goethe, six months before, was dangerously ill and his good friend Zelter, the composer, hurried to see him perhaps for the last time, he hesitated, as his diary reports, on the porch: 'Am I to leave again? Is this the dwelling-place of death?' But then he found one, 'who looked as if he suffered love, the whole of love with all the torments of youth. Well, if this is so, he will survive!'[5] Although this is undoubtedly a dramatization—for at that time it was not so much Goethe as the poem that suffered 'the whole of love'—it is yet appropriate that Goethe did, after all, have something to say about *Werther*, namely the verses 'To Werther', which later were to precede the 'Elegy' in the cycle of poems called 'Trilogy of Passion'.

> So once again, my shadow drowned in tears,
> You venture out into the light of day . . .

This is how it begins, and it ends with a variation on the words of Goethe's Tasso:

> *Und wenn der Mensch in seiner Qual verstummt,*
> *Gab mir ein Gott, zu sagen, wie ich leide. . . ,*

meaning that even when any other man would be *silenced* by despair, he, the poet, has been granted the gift of *saying* how he suffers. What is varied at the end of the poem addressed to the memory of Werther, is the Tasso affirmative. It becomes a prayer: May a god give him that power! And at the beginning of the 'Elegy' it would seem that the prayer has been granted: the 'Elegy' carries the motto from *Tasso* in its original form, that is, as an affirmation. Once more the poet has endured and survived the sufferings that caused the death of Werther. For just now—never mind the passage of fifty years, never mind the *Werther* jubilee!—just now Goethe had been Werther again.

In the fifty-second paragraph of the second part of *Parerga und Paralipomena*, Schopenhauer puts forward his thesis that the intellectual life of a man is ultimately not subject to the conditions of individual existence, but independent of what ordinarily constitutes life: the will and its passions—a thesis that is the very foundation of the philosopher's *magnum opus, The World as Will and Idea*; and as an example of such a separation he gives Goethe's conduct 'when in the midst of the war in the Champagne, he diligently observes phenomena that pertain to his theory of colours and, as soon as the fortress of Luxemburg affords him a few minutes of rest from the terrible misery of that campaign, he instantly immerses himself in his notebooks'.

In the month of October that followed upon the September of Goethe's parting with Ulrike—such parting as he called death in the poem 'To Werther'—Goethe, for the first time, showed the 'Elegy' to Eckermann—not without the most solemn preparation. He had placed two candles at the head of the fairest of fair copies written on pages of fine parchment 'that were fixed with a silken cord to covers made of moroccan leather'; and when Eckermann had finished reading, Goethe said '*Gelt*' —'*gelt*' is a smug, in Goethe's case no doubt Frankfurt dialect-coloured word, meaning 'well, ain't it so?'—'*Gelt*, have I not shown you something good?' We readily believe that he did say '*gelt*' and allow this comfortable little word to emphasize the 'separation' of which Schopenhauer speaks: the separation of the world of the poem from the world in which poems are not made but proudly shown, a separation that provides the perspective of these meditations. '*Gelt*, have I not shown you something good?'—namely the product of that 'very impassioned state' that in Goethe's biography is for ever associated with Marienbad.[6]

The summer of 1823 that Goethe spent in the Bohemian spas Marienbad and Karlsbad, for the third and last time near the much-loved girl, loved never more than during this last summer—what was it like? Before we turn towards the poet Goethe-Tasso and his agony, and the divine power which, through poetry, liberated that suffering from its muteness, we should like to imagine what occurred in 'reality'. Which reality? Well, the reality where people come and go, pack or unpack their luggage, settle down in hotel rooms, drink the health-giving water; where the sun rises, stands at high noon, and in setting ushers in the evening; where green shadows envelop the walkers in the woods and where the rich guests arrange parties and dances, as for instance Frau Rosalie von Geymüller, a Viennese banker's wife, whose Marienbad receptions Goethe used to attend: Goethe, or rather, as we speak of that reality, 'His Excellency Johann Wolfgang Goethe from Weimar, recipient of the gold medal of the Grand Duchy of Saxony, the Grand Duke's Counsellor and Minister of State', as the Marienbad guest register would have it with earnest solemnity; the reality, then, which even Metternich's secret police could reliably examine, the police who were kept very busy indeed by the presence in Marienbad of several foreign princes and politicians, and incessantly had to write reports to the government offices in Prague, like that about Frau Geymüller who, according to the police, scandalized the public by her 'conduct in general' and particularly by the 'insensible extravagance' of her attire: 'Three or even four times a day she would change her costume, each more expensive than the last . . . She makes no secret of the fact that she brought 150 such dresses to Marienbad'—the police had obviously counted them—'not

to mention more than 300 négligés.' 'As she never mixes with
women, but only with men, young men at that, it is easy to
account for the malicious remarks she elicits from the ladies
here.'[7]—This, then, was the Marienbad reality, inspected and
reported by the police.

Goethe himself did not see this reality very differently when,
on 18 July 1823, he wrote to his friend Knebel: 'The company
here is very good, one may even say: splendid. Beautiful
women can be seen in carriages, on horse-back or on foot, ever
so often there are dances, and if one wishes for more serious
conversations, there is no lack of wordly-wise diplomats or
other men of the world.' From Goethe's diaries and letters one
can reconstruct a calendar of pleasures which may appear
excessive to philistines as well as to prudent men: to philistines
because they are philistines and to prudent men because they
may think of Goethe's age as well as of the heart condition of
the past winter months when, as Goethe put it to Chancellor
von Müller, 'death lurked in every corner': 'There is something within me that stands in the way of my living or dying;
I wonder how it will end'—this is what the Chancellor heard
him say on 24 February 1823. But now in Marienbad? On
20 July a party where Goethe danced uninterruptedly for four
hours; on 24 July an 'improvised dance' and 'a little supper that
went on until midnight'; on the following day 'a social gather-
ing in the evening. Games being played'; on the next evening,
Count Klebelsberg himself plays the piano for the revellers.
In Goethe's letters to Weimar, time and again, he reports:
'The sound of champagne bottles being uncorked. It was past
midnight that I came home' or 'Leaps and gallopades as
usual...'[8] Certainly, it was the truth when on 12 July he replied
to a letter from his friend, Grüner, superintendent of the police
in near-by Eger and his fellow-researcher in mineralogy, who

had remarked that the Marienbad therapy seemed to do Goethe a lot of good: 'It isn't because of the therapy that I am visiting these spas; I am living here most agreeably, the clean air and the contact with interesting persons make my days most pleasurable.'

Indeed, it is a life of pleasure; and hardly anything prepares us for the seriousness very soon to be voiced by the poetry of the 'Elegy'; hardly anything, except perhaps a few faint allusions, in his gallant and coquettish poems written for Ulrike, to the dark sphere from which had arisen, in February 1823, his mysterious lament uttered to Chancellor von Müller, about 'the masses of pathological stuff' that have 'burdened me for three thousand years'; or the line that he wrote in his calendar for the year 1823 opposite the January page: 'I am imprisoned! As in a deep, deep tomb!' Or the four verses written in all probability at the same time:

> If only I could flee from myself!
> The cup is overfull.
> Why is it that I always strive
> For things not meant for me?

Yet it would be impossible to guess, from the innocuous little verses he made for Ulrike, at the 'impassioned state' the 'product' of which was the Marienbad 'Elegy'. True, on 18 August, one day after the Levetzows moved from Marienbad to Karlsbad, he wrote a letter to his daughter-in-law, Ottilie, which must have struck her as very strange: Marienbad, he wrote, is the place where, in the midst of the daily routine, in the whirl of all the distractions, 'there moves a will o' the wisp which leads one more and more deeply into the malady which one wanted to throw off. If in addition you imagine experiences recognized for what they were only after they have passed, then you may comprehend the bitter-sweet cup which I have emptied to its last dregs.' This very strange letter sounds a little like the four lines he wrote in that bad winter on the same sheet as the verses just quoted:

> Ah, if only one could be well again!
> What insufferable pains!
> Like a wounded serpent
> It turns and twists in one's heart.

On the very same day when he wrote that ominous letter to Ottilie, he also wrote into the album of the beautiful Polish pianist Szymanowska, whom he much admired, the first-born poem of the 'Trilogy of Passion'. It appeared twice in the final edition of his works that he supervised himself, *Die Ausgabe letzter Hand*, once as the poem that it was when it was written: homage to Szymanowska, and the second time, under the title 'Reconciliation', as the conclusion of the 'Trilogy of Passion' that begins with the evocation of Werther's memory and has as its centre the 'Elegy'. Strange, is it not? this conciliatory ending that originated before the tragedy and was later added as a postscript of harmony:

> *Da fühlte sich—o dass es ewig bliebe!—*
> *Das Doppel-Glück der Töne wie der Liebe;*

voicing the desire for the ever-lastingness of the twofold happiness of music and love.

And what was the 'reality' of Goethe's when he composed the 'Elegy'? If he was, as he himself said, in 'an impassioned state', then there obviously was no question of 'emotion re-collected in tranquillity', as Wordsworth defined the condition of the lyrical poet. No, such was certainly not the condition of the traveller in the horse-drawn carriage that on 5 September 1823, 'after a somewhat tumultuous farewell', as the diary

reports, left Karlsbad in the direction of Weimar. It was the
very coach in which one of the most celebrated poems in all
literature came into being. One ought to imagine the situation
as exactly as possible, not only for the sake of the poem but of
poetics too.

Well, then: Goethe, in the course of that summer, hopelessly
surrendered to a hopeless passion: he was seventy-four and
she nineteen. In the preceding winter, we know, he had almost
died. He slowly recovered, but remained in low spirits. 'I am
not well', he had complained the year before, 'because I am
not in love with anyone, and nobody is in love with me.'[9]
Madame de Staël had once said of him that for his well-being
he needed the intrigues of seduction. It would be even truer to
say that he needed amours in order to allow life to seduce him.
In *Wilhelm Meister* he said: 'Life amounts to nothing if the one
thing is lacking that is worth more than all the rest.'[10] Now he
was in love again. If it was a will-o'-the-wisp, it was love
all the same. Two stanzas of the 'Elegy' describe what was
before and what was now; before: deep anxiety oppressing
mind and body alike, terrifying visions from the empty heart
that knew no love, knew not even that it was in need of it; and
now: *vita nuova*:

> *Wenn Liebe je den Liebenden begeistet,*
> *Ward es an mir aufs lieblichste geleistet;*
>
> *Und zwar durch sie!*

Thanks to her there was life again, and the inspiration to live
and work.

He went so far as to propose marriage. Mother and daughter
gently rejected the proposal, probably so gently that he believed
that there was still hope. 'The family', as he always referred to
the Levetzows in his diary, left Marienbad after this incident,

probably to remove themselves from the scene of the embarrassment—not very far, it is true: to nearby Karlsbad, and not
without the promise of a future meeting. This was on 17
August. His diary of 20 August contains the entry: 'A quiet
night. Conciliatory dreams.' Never before or afterwards had
anyone made such dreamy use of the word '*konziliant*'. On
23 August Goethe himself left Marienbad, first for Eger to visit
his friend Grüner. On his way there he stops again and again
and 'hammers away', as with mineralogical meticulousness the
diary remembers. He is above all after 'undulatory slate rich in
flint' and 'pyrotypical stone of several kinds'. From Eger he
sends Ulrike a little poem. As she dwells entirely in his heart,
it says, it is difficult for him to comprehend how she can possibly
be elsewhere.[11] The other stone-splitter, Grüner, the superintendent of the Eger police, suggests that he should spend his
approaching birthday at the castle of Count Auersperg, but did
not succeed in persuading him. Goethe pretended that his
presence in Karlsbad was necessary. He went there on 25
August. Gossip had caught up with him. There is a letter
preserved that a baron from Riga wrote home: 'Goethe too is
here. They say that his only reason is a pair of beautiful eyes . . .
en route in Karlsbad. Confident of his immortality, he now,
in his seventh decade, sets out on a new career. Collecting
minerals in Marienbad, he picked up an hitherto unknown
heart violet . . . In brief, he is in love with a young girl; he is
beside himself; he wants to marry her. What poetic frenzy!'[12]
It obviously was the most delicious scandal of the Karlsbad
season.

   Small wonder that the rumours reached Weimar where
Goethe's son and daughter-in-law became the more agitated
as Goethe himself, cautiously and mysteriously, had hinted
at possible changes in their domestic arrangements. He wrote

to them: 'The living together of such good and reasonable
people as we are has been at times as difficult as can be; what is
lacking is a third or fourth person to close the circle.' The
epistle was signed: 'Your—in the most beautiful sense—loving
father.'[13] Despite the unfortunate Marienbad proposal, it was
with such thoughts in his heart that he arrived in Karlsbad. He
would not take rooms in his usual place but moved into the
same house as the Levetzows. The diary entry of the first day
ends: 'Spent the evening with the family. The waning moon
rising brightly above the Threecross Mountain.'[14]

August 28 arrived, his birthday. Goethe believed he could
keep 'the family' in the dark about the day. Without mentioning the occasion, he arranged an excursion. When he came
down for breakfast, he found in his place a cup on which a
garland of ivy was painted. Ulrike herself, in her old age, has
narrated it all very affectingly. 'Why the pretty cup?', Goethe
asked. 'To remind you of our friendship. Ivy is its symbol',
said Frau von Levetzow. At the picnic she presented him with a
glass on which her name was engraved and those of her three
daughters: 'Despite it all'—no doubt she alluded to the rejected
proposal—'we don't want to be forgotten. Remember us
always and also this occasion.' This is what, according to
Ulrike, her mother said. It sounds like farewell, but Goethe
remained in a serene mood. Next morning Goethe's first
question was: 'You did know, didn't you, that yesterday was
my birthday?' Mother replied: 'How should I not? After all,
you allowed it to be printed.' 'Well, then', he said, 'let's call
it the day of the public secret.'[15]

The following days were very much like those in Marienbad:
social events and mineralogical diversions: 'Basalt and columnar
iron-stone.' Once Ulrike read to him from a book. He seems
detached enough to criticize her reading in the diary: '. . . on

the whole well and without affectation, but she ought to read with more energy and vivacity.'[16] On the morning of 15 September he departs after that 'somewhat tumultuous farewell'. As early as the luncheon-break he begins to write down a poem that he had composed in his mind while travelling: it is the beginning of the 'Elegy' the regular rhythm of which—it consists of slightly modified Italian stanzas—seems to reflect the movement of the carriage rolling along the country road:

> *Was soll ich nun von Wiedersehen hoffen,*
> *Von dieses Tages noch geschlossner Blüte?*

The constellation envisaged in the poem is a meeting with the beloved and the tormenting uncertainty of the lover's reception, although there seems nothing but sure hope, a hope fulfilled at the end of the stanza, in the image of the still-closed blossom of daybreak. None the less, the outcome is unsure: Is Hell awaiting him? Heaven? But all doubts vanish as she appears at the gates of Paradise and beckons him to follow.—Amazing, the vitality of an imagination capable of holding up before the defeated soul the hope, indeed the certainty of such a blissful reunion! Or has this parting of the imagination from the soul and its passions deeper causes?

In the thirty-sixth paragraph of the first volume of Schopenhauer's *World as Will and Idea*, genius, the genius of art, is defined as 'perfect objectivity', as the fullest realization of the exceptional mind's ability to cut itself loose from its 'subjective' tendencies, from the interest the individual takes in himself, the aims of its will and passions. Genius consists in the faculty of 'pure contemplation', the power of the mind to transcend its self-interest and to lose itself entirely in the vision of the object to be represented, indeed 'to disown for some time one's own personality and exist alone for the sake of knowledge, as a medium of lucid vision'. This talent—the very talent of genius —becomes the more sublime the closer it approaches the person's own 'subjectivity', making the self and its emotions the object of the poetic 'objectivity'. For in this manner the self's very pain and suffering is 'for some time' redeemed through 'pure contemplation' and anaesthetized, as it were, in the 'lucid vision' of the poem. It is, in this case, passion itself that ceases to be passion's slave; but meanwhile, as Schopenhauer puts it, it is 'the poet himself that pays the price for the performance of this spectacle'.

It is through the two 'realities', one in which Goethe's 'Elegy' is domiciled and the other which shows in his ordinary and extra-poetic circumstances and utterances during that Bohemian summer, that we are led to Schopenhauer's important theory of art, important not only in itself but because—in strange contrast to its present neglect—it deeply impressed so many artists even if they never came into immediate contact with it. For Schopenhauer's doctrine bases itself on a dichotomy that has been ever more acutely felt by artists of the 'prosaic age' (as Goethe himself once called it),[17] the gulf between the artist's self in the world as it is experienced day by day, and the other reality of the work or the poem; the world, on the one hand, in which one collects basalt and iron-stone, arranges birthday picnics, indulges in flirtatious small-talk at the dances of the extravagant Frau Geymüller; and on the other hand, the world of the silent agony which the poet 'objectifies', redeeming it in language; for instance thus:

> *Schon rast's und reisst in meiner Brust gewaltsam,*
> *Wo Tod und Leben sich bekämpfen.*
> *Wohl Kräuter gäb's, des Körpers Qual zu stillen:*
> *Allein dem Geist fehlt's an Entschluss und Willen . . .*

verses which are about the struggle between life and death raging within, and the irresolution, the cowardice, of a mind that does not end it all by making use of the deadly offerings of pharmacology.

But the diary of the journey home speaks of walks, of agriculture, black-lead spar, minerals sorted out after lunch with Superintendent Grüner, lively conversations about the mineralogy and geology of Bohemia, a visit to the Eger pharmacy. Disrespect tempts one to ask: To enquire into its store of poison? By no means: to consult the weather-glass. And then again: 'work on the poem', the very poem in which a desperate man bids his friends to leave him alone with his suffering—one makes no mistake by imagining Herr Grüner as one of those friends—, the poem that puts all the botanical, mineralogical, meteorological inquisitiveness into its place: a place reduced to triviality by the soul's agony. This is what the verses say:

> *Verlasst mich hier, getreue Weggenossen!*
> *Lasst mich allein am Fels, in Moor und Moos;*
> *Nur immer zu! Euch ist die Welt erschlossen,*
> *Die Erde weit, der Himmel hehr und gross;*
> *Betrachtet, forscht, die Einzelheiten sammelt,*
> *Naturgeheimnis werde nachgestammelt.*
> *Mir ist das All, ich bin mir selbst verloren . . .*

'*Naturgeheimnis werde nachgestammelt*'—'Continue, if you like with your stuttering and stammering attempts to conjure up the mystery of Nature!' The measure of desperation yielded by this line is beyond comprehension. Goethe speaks here with the utmost contempt of what often enough he regarded as the task of his life, more important even than his poetry: to let Nature herself speak, to lend her his words, and thus help man to gain some insight into her dark designs. And *when* was this stanza, beginning with 'Leave me now, loyal companions of my journeying'—when was it written? Perhaps on the very same day on which, according to the diary, he conversed in the most vivacious manner about the mineralogy and geology of Bohemia. And the stanza's contrast between the desperate man, who is lost to himself and the world, and those others who enjoy living in the world, is of course expressed not only in words that simply say so but through poetry: on the one hand the dramatic monologue delivered with convincing contempt by one who has experienced his private apocalypse, and, on the other, the description of life lived by those who enjoy it, don't know the depth of the poet's misery and would not understand it. Yet no sooner has the poet begun to describe their world, than it ceases to be a world petty and trivial, a world that would shrivel into nothingness before the great passion. No, it is the earth wide and alluring, a firmament '*hehr und gross*', majestic and grand. Does this not give the lie to the dark apocalypse, does it not show the imagination of a poet still capable of being carried away by the splendour of the world—of the very same world which, as the rest of his speech will have it, has come to mean nothing to him?

This strange contradiction between the self of the poet, in his present misery contemptuous of the world, and the same poet's poem is even more conspicuous in another stanza of the 'Elegy'. Indeed, that stanza is hardly inferior to Goethe's most magnificent panegyrics of '*das Naturschöne*', of natural beauty, youthful evocations, for instance, of the luminous splendour of a spring day ('*Wie herrlich leuchtet mir die Natur*'), or his thanks-givings in *Faust I* to the great spirit of Nature that had granted him every wish ('*Erhabner Geist, du gabst mir, gabst mir alles*'); or the dithyrambs that accompany Faust's awakening at the beginning of *Faust II* in a world restored to youth and beauty every morning. According to the monologue sense of those verses of the 'Elegy' it is an unhappy man, ready to die, who asks, vainly trying to comfort himself, whether the world is really no longer there, the world which once he knew was beautiful but now appears to have abandoned him. But he asks in such a manner as, in poetic reality, only a happy man would be able to ask, hymnic even in the cadences of questioning:

> *Ist denn die Welt nicht übrig? Felsenwände,*
> *Sind sie nicht mehr gekrönt von heiligen Schatten?*
> *Die Ernte, reift sie nicht? Ein grün Gelände,*
> *Zieht sich's nicht hin an Fluss und Busch und Matten?*
> *Und wölbt sich nicht das überweltlich Grosse,*
> *Gestaltenreiche, bald Gestaltenlose?*

Like all great lyrical poetry it is untranslatable. Still, the desperate question is: What has happened to the world? Has it not changed beyond recognition? The walls of rock along the river, are they no longer crowned, as if by haloes, with the rainbows the sun forms in the watery atmosphere? Will the fields not be ready soon for the harvesters? Are there not meadows that, through clumps of trees and bushes, follow the winding course of the river? And is not, greater than anything, the sky vaulting above this scene, the sky forming and then again unforming its cloudy shapes?

It is unbelievable and seems impossible; the drama of the 'Elegy' would demand that the answers to these questions—questions only in accordance with their grammatical form, but according to their meaning exclamations of enchantment—should be *no*, or at least: all this is no longer for him. But who is the questioner in his travelling carriage that follows the road from Karlsbad towards the Bavarian frontier along steep drops of rock and then again through meadows stretching along the

river or between fields where the harvest waits to be garnered
in these early September days? Indeed, who asks these questions?
Or rather: who praises, be it only in the form of questions, the
earth, the sun, the sky, the clouds? One who, while he makes
poetry, is once again *enraptured* by the words and images that
his experience of the universe offers to him, or one who,
because his love has abandoned him, must also forgo, as he
laments, the word-bliss of his feelings for Nature? That a man,
in well-wrought stanzas says what he suffers, he himself,
lyrically, in his own person, is by itself full of problems,
although one usually makes no fuss about them. And all these
problems concern the relationship between the empirical and
the aesthetic reality. But even more puzzling is the case of a
poet who puts the abundant splendour of undeniably authentic
evocations of Nature at the service of his intention to say that
in his wretchedness he has become incapable of feeling any of it.
Comparing with these verses of the 'Elegy' those that Shakespeare puts into the mouth of his Hamlet to express his *taedium
vitae*, we find that the hero's weariness colours every image. Life
itself withers as soon as the eyes of the unhappy man are set on
it:

> How weary, stale, flat, and unprofitable
> Seem to me all the uses of this world!
> Fie on't, ah fie, 'tis an unweeded garden
> That grows to seed. Things rank and gross in nature
> Possess it . . .

But in Goethe's lyrical rejection of life there is, on the contrary,
a blossoming and glowing to make even the question-marks
radiant with affirmation.

'In every great separation there lies a seed of madness; one
has to be careful not to foster its growth', we read in Goethe's

Maxims and Reflections;[18] and in his poem 'To Werther', the first of the 'Trilogy of Passion', such partings are compared to death itself. There is no other poem that is as eloquent as the 'Elegy' in urging upon the reader the problem of the relationship prevailing between the man who suffers the passion and the poet who turns it to poetry. Certainly, it has been said very concisely: 'SPRICHT *die Seele, so spricht, ach, schon die* SEELE *nicht mehr*';[19] 'as soon as the soul begins to *speak*, the speech, alas, is no longer the *soul's*', certainly not of the speechless soul, that much is self-evident; and although the making of poetry is merely a particular instance of the soul's speaking, it is yet a *very* particular instance: because of the aesthetic character of poetic speech which maintains the most complex relations with the spontaneity of feelings. Poetry is the language of those feelings—and therefore in the *literal* sense the feelings themselves; but at the same time it is to feelings (or, for that matter, thoughts) what chisel and marble are to the sculptor's inner vision. But with this, we have returned to Schopenhauer.

This philosopher insists, as we have seen, upon the strict separation of what he calls Will, meaning by this above all the passions—for instance the impassioned state of the old man in Marienbad in love with the young girl—the strict separation, then, of will, desire and passion from that pure contemplation that raises soul and mind above the Will and its aims, a contemplative power that is at its most powerful in genius. Schopenhauer says so in *The World as Will and Idea*, and so say in one way or another all those who after him—and more often than not without having read him—proclaim the absolute autonomy of *artistic* experience and procedure, the independence of art of the 'will-full' self's emotions, thoughts, or moods. This separation is most conspicuous in the doctrine of '*poésie pure*' and, even without any regard to theory or aesthetic philosophy, it can be followed from Baudelaire through Mallarmé to Valéry, from Rilke or George to Benn, or with a difference, from Thomas Mann's *Tonio Kröger* through T. S. Eliot to the practitioners of the 'New Criticism', now no longer quite so new. Without any prompting by Schopenhauer, Rilke, for instance, speaks of the 'great artist's gaze' that 'desires nothing'; and at those times when Goethe did not look upon his writings as fragments of a great personal confession, he showed the same awareness as Rilke when, for instance, in his *Torquato Tasso* he says of Homer that *in utter self-forgetfulness* he dedicated his life to the contemplation of two heroes, Achilles and Ulysses.

Whether Schopenhauer's philosophy of art is conclusive or not, it certainly carried conviction. Its dogma of the complete 'otherness' of artistic creativity, of the total divorce of the mode of art from man's mode of existing in what one customarily regards as 'real' life, the elevation of the common-sense differ-ence between the prosaic talk of everyday and the speech of poetry to the rank of a metaphysical principle, is rooted in the firm belief of the pessimistic philosopher, shared by so many, that the world as it is, before art has transformed and ennobled it, is worth nothing and an offence to the spirit. Is it true to say that such pessimism was as alien to Goethe as is commonly assumed? Certainly not in all seasons of his life, and most certainly not if the last stanza of the 'Elegy' is confessional even to the slightest degree. For it contains the declaration of abysmal defeat: he is abandoned by the world and lost to him-self after the gods took away from him what first they gave him: Pandora, as rich in blessings as in dangers:

> *Sie drängten mich zum gabenseligen Munde,*
> *Sie trennen mich—und richten mich zu Grunde.*

In this parting there is more than 'a seed of madness'; it means perdition. And late in his life, looking back upon it, he thought he had experienced, all in all, perhaps four weeks of happiness; and once he asked himself how a man who at the age of 22 had so clearly seen the absurdity of existence as he had done in *Werther*, still could want to live at 72.[20] 'I daresay', he remarked to Zelter in 1812, 'I could write a new Werther that, even more than the first, would make people's hair stand on end.'[21] He was 63 then; and in 1816, after he had read *Werther* again, he observed: 'It has been only my talent that has made me endure all these conditions that are contrary to my nature.'[22] With this we are certainly close to Schopenhauer's aesthetic pessimism and find ourselves in the very middle of it when beholding the intriguing fellowship of the bliss of words and the despair of love that characterizes the 'Elegy'.

It contains a stanza—beginning with the line '*Wie leicht und zierlich, klar und zart gewoben*' (never before have clarity and tenderness been so happily married)—where the deserted lover imagines he espies the beloved, 'the loveliest of all most lovely forms', a slender thing made of the fragrance of light, in the dance of clouds against the blueness of the sky. But this illusion of the *outer* world is instantly rejected in a verse which—to one who has been preoccupied, perhaps too long, with Hegel and Rilke—makes it impossible not to be reminded of Hegel's prophecy that an epoch was approaching in which all 'significant reality' would recede into the *inwardness* of human subjectivity; or Rilke's Duino-Muzot annunciation that, as the comprehensible external reality is more and more deserted by meaning, 'world' would truly exist only 'within'.

Are such associations forbidden? Do such ominous and perhaps eccentric forebodings come from regions very different from those inhabited by Goethe's poetry? The answer is yes, if Goethe's ever-repeated emphasis upon the significance of the concrete particular in the domain of external phenomena is made into a dogma of wordly piety. Yet the indisputable evidence shows that even he experienced at times, within himself, what was revealed to his Tasso: that the fine fabric of his poetry was like the silkworm's cocoon: his coffin in which he shut himself off from 'life'. And with this we have almost arrived at what Kafka said of his heaven knows, very different —literary work when he tried to persuade his fiancée that she must not marry him: for he did not exist 'in reality'; he lived only in the reality of his writings; but his writing was done in a sleep deeper still than the deepest sleep, that is: death. But now we are indeed far away from Goethe: a hundred years; and this is in some respects a very long time, but in others like yesterday.

It is only for a few minutes that the cloud lasts, the airy shape in which the poet of the 'Elegy' recognized 'the loveliest of all most lovely forms'. (It is, in every sense, a superlative poem in which the very last kiss, '*der letzteste*', follows upon the last.) And as the wind dissolves the clouds, reality itself becomes an airy thing, the signal for the lover's mind and imagination, defeated and yet suddenly victorious, to retreat into his inmost heart: '*Ins Herz zurück*'. It is there, within, that he will truly find what he seeks, the one and only one whose image none the less merges with all those who have ever been loved by this lover.

The retreat into inwardness, not only from the outer reality of cloudy, airy shapes: two months later, on 4 November 1823 (we are still in the year of the 'Elegy'), Goethe was to say it again, this time in prose, the prose of Chancellor von Müller's memory of the occasion. Weimar gave a farewell party to Maria Szymanowska, the graceful and accomplished pianist from Poland, who very probably was one of 'all those who have ever been loved by this lover'. Chancellor Müller knew this.

As early as 25 September 1823 he had written to Julie von Egloffstein about Goethe's relationship to Szymanowska: 'And so you can see that his passion for Ulrike von Levetzow is at least not exclusive, and that I am right in asserting that it was not this particular girl who has brought about the present state of mind, but the enhanced need of his soul for communication and sympathy.' At that *soirée* for Maria Szymanowska someone toasted remembrance; for it was in the memory of her Weimar friends that the celebrated guest would stay on with them. The toast was not to Goethe's liking. He replied:

To speak of remembrance as you do is merely a clumsy way of expressing oneself. Whenever we have experienced something great or beautiful or significant, it need not be recalled as if it were recaptured from without. On the contrary, it must from the very beginning become interwoven with our inner being, become one with it, make us into a new and better person and thus creatively live on for ever within ourselves. We must not long for the return of anything that has passed: in a sense, there is no past; there is only the ever new that is formed from the elements of what we call the past; longing must always be creative . . .

And greatly moved, he added: 'Have we not learned it in these days?'—learned it, we may well ask, from Ulrike or Maria Szymanowska?—'This lovable and noble person who is about to leave us now, has she not rejuvenated our inmost being, made it better and greater? No, she cannot vanish again, she has become joined to our inner nature, she will live on with us, and whatever she may do in the future, she cannot flee from me, I am holding her fast within myself.' This is how she (who *is* she? Szymanowska? Ulrike?) became married to his inmost self. This is how his longing proved genuine and 'creative'—by producing something 'better and greater': a poem.

'*Du hast gut reden.*' 'It is easy for you to talk'—these words from the 'Elegy' suggest themselves, words that, as often happens in great poetry, strangely elevate the lowlands of the vernacular. 'It is easy for you to talk.' For who at that party was able to understand what Goethe meant, let alone act upon it 'within'? This kind of 'holding fast' is what Goethe had already practised during those August days in Marienbad. And so it is, after all, not all that puzzling that he placed the poem in homage of Maria Szymanowska at the end of the 'Trilogy of Passion' under the title of 'Reconciliation'. 'It is easy for you to talk': for only the poet has the power so perfectly to 'internalize' the outer event, to accommodate so happily in the inner spaces the exiles from the external world, a process which it would certainly be 'clumsy' simply to call 'remembrance'. (This is also the reason why 'Remembrance of Things Past', although it comes from Shakespeare, is so wrong a title for Proust's *magnum opus*; and how Goethe's little oration against the simple-minded 'rememberers' would have delighted Proust!) This, then, is how the world, in which the poet's self, the creature of the Will, moves as if in a labyrinth, is transformed into an 'objective' possession, a state of the self's mind, a poem in which even this very same self with all its passions can be quietly contemplated as if it were reflected in a lake, plaything of wind and light and poetry.

If we accept Schopenhauer's philosophy of art, shall we find a place in it at all for the lyrical poet? Does he not use all the time the little word that, according to Schopenhauer, is taboo to the artist, the word 'I,' as, for instance, William Blake does thrice in the lines:

> and in melodious accents I
> Will sit me down and Cry I, I.

The question was asked by the young author of *The Birth of*

Tragedy, Nietzsche. He knew that Schopenhauer, in his aesthetic philosophy, did not feel at ease when he thought of the lyrical poet who gives us 'fragments of a great confession' or sings to us 'the whole chromatic scale of his passions and desires'. Nietzsche, at that time still deeply devoted to the pessimistic philosopher, came to his rescue by taking the lyrical 'I' out of the world of ordinary I-experiences, raising it to the height of the Platonic ideas. The 'I' of the successful lyrical poem is not identical with the empirico-biographical 'I' of the poet. In the act of poetic creation it frees itself, Nietzsche writes, of his individual will and turns itself into a mere medium, in which and through which it finds its redemption by contemplating and uttering the *idea* of itself. This is the miraculous 'I'-condition in which the poet is, in Nietzsche's words, 'like that fabulous creature in the fairytale that can turn its eyes in such a way that he can look at himself. Now he is at once subject and object, poet, actor and spectator, all at the same time.' In other words, which are almost Nietzsche's *and* Goethe's words: through the poem the poet's self becomes an 'aesthetic phenomenon', as Nietzsche calls it in *The Birth of Tragedy*, saying of it that it is the *only justification* of world and existence, and now, by implication, also of the human person.[23] (Surprisingly early in his life, in 1777, Goethe said of himself, in a letter to Frau von Stein: 'You know how symbolic my existence is . . .'). The 'I' of the poem, as subject *and* object of lyrical contemplation, begins to speak only when the 'merely'-human 'I' has come to an end:

> *Und wenn der Mensch in seiner Qual verstummt,*
> *Gab mir ein Gott zu sagen, wie ich leide . . .*

It is a god who has given the poet the power to speak where man is silenced by his agony. This god is undoubtedly the same who has created the world as the aesthetic phenomenon, a world,

that is, of which Nietzsche held that it stood in no need of any
further justification, while the 'real' world, the artistically
'speechless' world, cannot be vindicated. (The tremendous
tension that exists between this aesthetic philosophy and an
ethically determined religion is demonstrated by Kierkegaard.
In his dissertation *About the Concept of Irony* he praised Goethe
for 'bringing together his existence as a poet with the reality of
his life', but later, in his *Stages on the Way through Life*, he makes
Goethe the paradigm for the 'aesthetic falsification' of existence:
'As soon as any situation in life threatened to gain the upper
hand, he escaped from it by turning it into a poem.' Yet to
remove oneself from 'the scene of reality' through poetry,
'means to falsify the ethical nature of human reality . . .'[24]

Not since Dante has there been a love poem as rich as the
'Elegy' in theological vocabulary. The gates of Paradise as well
as Hell stand open; the beloved appears at the door of Paradise
to welcome the lover as if to let him partake in eternal life,
then the angel with the flaming sword drives him away and the
gates close behind him; to be loved by her is compared to God's
peace that passes understanding. God's peace: as long as forty-
eight years before the 'Elegy' in 1775, when his love's name
was Lili, Goethe knew that his manner of suffering the ever-
recurring torments of love rose from an unquiet heart which
no fulfilment on earth could possibly assuage. This is what his
poem '*Sehnsucht*' says. Its rhythm is derived from the church
hymn 'O Father of Mercy': if only the merciful Father, the
poem says, would quieten the poet's soul by filling it with
His presence! But there should also be love—this poet's
love. It is a prayer for what in Goethe's case is mutually
exclusive. Is the divine absence the reason why he loved as he
loved? Why he was driven as if by a demon from '*Liebschaft*'
to '*Liebschaft*', and time and again to loves where even the

external circumstances made sure that they remained unrealized: to Charlotte Buff who was promised to another, to Charlotte von Stein and Marianne Willemer who were married, to Ulrike who was impossibly young? But the external obstacle is merely a *chiffre* of the very nature of such romantic loving, of its nature or its lack of nature or its being 'out of nature'. It seems of its essence that it cannot be realized in a reality that unavoidably is unresponsive to its demands. Werther does not 'really' want his Lotte as wife nor Tasso his princess. What in *Faust II* the *mater gloriosa* calls out to that penitent 'who used to be called Gretchen': namely that she should lift herself up to higher spheres where Faust is bound to follow her, applies, in one way or another, to all the beloved in all the great romantic love poems, from Dante's *Vita nuova* to Goethe's 'Elegy'; but the 'higher sphere', for lack of maps or definitions, became ever less accessible in the course of history.

Not to Dante. The Thomist Christian endowed this knowledge with permanence. His Inferno as well as his Paradise have a theological solidity that is missing from the purely poetic symbols, the Paradise and Hell of Goethe's 'Elegy'. It was Goethe's historical fate that his sensibility, nourished from the deepest soil of Romanticism, needed the *reality* of transcendence, yet experienced only its intimations in the flights and falls of his loves or in the raptures of the poetic imagination. There indeed, and ever anew, he learned the lesson that all the passing things of this world are symbols—'*Alles Vergängliche ist nur ein Gleichnis*'—symbols that in other ages—after all, Goethe himself alluded to the Father of Mercy—had the quality of the sacramental. Goethe spoke of 'the instantaneous revelation of the unfathomable'.[25] This is how he once defined the symbol, this impossible or only rarely attainable reconciliation of the 'real' with something we call 'sense' or 'meaning'; of concrete existence with that which points beyond it. 'How foolish', Goethe wrote to Zelter on 19 October 1829, when no doubt his anger was once again roused by the Transcendental Idealists of his Germany: '. . . how foolish that the Real is, as it were, cancelled out by the Ideal. This may well be the reason why modern man knows the Ideal only in his longing (*'Nur als Sehnsucht'*) . . . But the most wonderful thing of antiquity is the health of the moment . . . Its products allow us to feel that the moment must be significant and sufficient in itself.' This 'health' of antiquity explains perhaps what is meant when at about the same time he darkly spoke of the 'masses of pathological stuff' that have oppressed him 'for three thousand years'.

His mind was such that he could not but seek such 'health' in the eternalized moment. Sometimes he succeeded: in the poetry of the 'Elegy', for instance. During the dangerous illness he suffered in the late autumn of 1823, he asked his friend Zelter every so often to read this poem to him. The candles were lighted when the precious possession was brought to the table. It was as if Mass were celebrated. Goethe recovered. Perhaps it was this prescription that helped.

> *Was einmal war in allem Glanz und Schein,*
> *Es regt sich dort, denn es will ewig sein.*

These lines occur in *Faust II*—and mean that there is a sphere where everything that had once attained splendour and beauty is still alive: for its very nature is the desire to be eternal. But something—was it his historical situation or the notorious 'other soul' in his breast?—prompted him to write into the margin of this eternity: 'And yet it vanishes.' This skirmish between the poetic text and the marginal gloss provides the measure of Goethe's profound irony even more clearly than the two realities of Marienbad.

II

Nietzsche in the Waste Land

Thus Spoke Zarathustra (1883–5) is, among Nietzsche's works, the book on which, for a long time, his fame rested most massively as if on a throne designed by some *art nouveau* or *Jugendstil* artist; and if Nietzsche himself conceived of his bearded prophet in the image of Leonardo da Vinci's red chalk self-portrait in Turin, the likeness, as it turned out, was more in the manner of a Pre-Raphaelite painter. Yet Nietzsche looked upon his *Zarathustra* as the Fifth Gospel, the gospel to take back, indeed obliterate, the preceding four, and held it to be the truest child of his poetic-philosophical genius. In his autobiography of 1888, *Ecce Homo*, the very title of which betrays the incipient delusion of grandeur and which none the less, in the passionate brilliance and precision of its language, bears witness to his genius (a great mind's megalomania—what a catastrophic superfluity!)—in *Ecce Homo* he records the upheaval of the spirit which, five years earlier, accompanied the birth of the First Part of *Zarathustra*. Is there anyone, Nietzsche asks in his autobiography, who, living at the end of the nineteenth century has a clear notion of what poets of poetically more powerful epochs called inspiration? 'Well, I shall describe it.' It is such that, if there were the slightest vestige of superstition in a man thus inspired, he would hardly be able to avoid believing that he was an incarnation, a mouthpiece, a medium of superior powers. 'Revelation'—the word used to convey the sense of something suddenly becoming visible that had not been seen before—would, he writes, be no exaggerated name for what he experienced. For he suddenly found what he had not searched for, and took, without asking whence it came, what offered itself. Luminous thoughts 'struck like lightning, their form predetermined by necessity, leaving no room for hesitation—I had no choice'.[1]

Although in reading and re-reading *Zarathustra* one wishes time and again that there had been less lightning and more hesitation, less necessity and more discretion, and above all less of that dialect of eternity which, like the eagle and the serpent and all the other evangelical, emblematic, and allegorical equipment, has sadly aged in excess of its years (while, to take only one example, the idiom of *Human, All-Too-Human* grows fresher with every reading), it is yet true to say that more often than not the radiance of Nietzsche's mind succeeds in penetrating its heavy prophetic attire, and sometimes even gains force by its parabolic presentation. Indeed, it happens that this or that tableau from *Zarathustra* does, despite those impediments, deliver its meaning with a directness unattainable by any discursive philosophizing. Take for instance Zarathustra's speech—it is his first—on 'The Three Metamorphoses' (even if its beginning comes close to an allegorical disaster):

Of three metamorphoses of the spirit I tell you: how the spirit becomes a camel; and the camel, a lion, and the lion, finally, a child.[2]

True, in trying to imagine these all-but unimaginable transformations it is hard to suppress a sense of extreme zoological and spiritual discomfort: Would, one wonders, the spirit not feel rather degraded by having to turn into a camel and would the lion not resist the operation that incongruously forces him into so helpless a human shape? Still, the prophet's inspiration becomes more convincing in what follows, probably because of the inconsistent but less demanding '*like* a camel' now replacing the full presence of the beast's symbolic reality. There is, we read, a stage in the spirit's voyage when it desires nothing more than to test its ability to bear heavy burdens, 'kneels down like a camel waiting to be well loaded' and asks for the most difficult* that 'I may take it upon myself and exult in my strength'. But what is the most difficult, the spirit inquires? To humble oneself to wound one's pride? To let one's folly shine in order to mock one's wisdom? Abandoning one's cause in the hour of its triumph? Climbing high mountains to tempt the tempter?'

Or is it this: feeding on the acorns and grass of knowledge and, for the sake of the truth, suffering hunger in one's soul?

Or is it this: being sick and sending home the comforters and making friends with the deaf, who never hear what you want?

Or is it this: stepping into filthy waters when they are the waters of truth, and not repulsing cold frogs and hot toads?

Or is it this: loving those who despise us and offering a hand to the ghost that would frighten us?

All these most difficult things the spirit that would bear much takes upon itself: like the camel that, burdened, speeds into the desert, thus the spirit speeds into its desert.[3]

If the inspiration that produced this had been as successful in its literary effect as it was powerful in Nietzsche's experience; and if it had brought about, as Nietzsche obviously wished it should, the fusion of both thought and experience into a great poetic parable, it would be petty and mean to dissolve it again into the elements from which it was made. As it is, no impiety

* The translation too is here 'most difficult', indeed impossible. For the German word is '*schwer*' which means both 'heavy', the right adjective for the camel's load, and 'difficult', the proper designation for the spirit's task. There is no English word that conveys the German double meaning.

is involved if one disregards for a little the animalistic metamorphoses of the spirit and speaks of Nietzsche himself, of his
personal and intellectual life—two biographical aspects that
are, with him, more intimately related than in the case of many
another philosopher. He knew this himself even though, as was
his wont, he instantly translated the personal insight into a
universal one: All philosophy, he said and implied again and
again, is in one sense or another autobiographical, for what dis-
tinguishes the philosopher from the 'scholar' or scientist is that
there is 'nothing whatever impersonal about him', his thinking
testifying at every point to 'who he is'.[4] (Could Aristotle have
said this? St Thomas Aquinas? Kant? Hardly. But Plato, yes;
and possibly St Augustine, and undoubtedly Pascal or Kierkegaard. This may well mark the point of departure for a
typology of thought and thinkers.)

If *Zarathustra* is a philosophical work, then Nietzsche's
equation of philosophy and autobiography is certainly applic-
able to this first speech of the philosopher-prophet; so much so
that it would not be unthinkable to write a Life of Nietzsche
as of one born under the sign of 'the Camel'. 'Lonely and
deeply suspicious of myself . . . , I took . . . sides *against* myself
and *for* anything that happened to hurt me and was hard for
me',[5] he said, and it was the fundamental truth of his existence,
from beginning to end and not only before Zarathustra
assigned to the spirit a career that took it beyond the stage of
the camel. Indeed, we should be mistaken if we assumed that
Nietzsche himself believed he had passed all the tests of Zarathustra's metamorphoses: camel, lion, child. Far from it, and
if he wished to *show* Zarathustra as one who had done so,
he did not succeed, for it is certainly neither a lion, rid of
scruples, nor a child, free of self-consciousness, that, to give only
one example, accuses the poets of lying too much and then,

defeated by his self-knowledge, says: 'But Zarathustra too is a poet. . . . *We* do lie too much'.[6] (Should not the lion ask. 'Why not lie?' He does not. On the contrary, the words convey, if not opprobrium, at least metaphysical discomfort or, worse still, Zarathustra's inability to believe in himself.)

Nor is it true to say that the thought of these metamorphoses 'struck like lightning' or was found without search. It had been, as a note from the time before *Zarathustra* shows, conscientiously rehearsed. Nietzsche, in that posthumous note,[7] does not yet speak of three transformations, but of '*drei Gänge*', three stages on the way, and does not clothe his meanings in symbols, but merely points to three different attitudes of mind and soul; and although the lines separating the three stages are not yet drawn as energetically as in Zarathustra's first speech, the sameness of the journey is yet discernible. To excel in admiring others, in obeying and learning, is the characteristic of the first stage, to 'assume heavy burdens', to allow oneself to be torn apart by contradictory devotions and to cultivate altogether a radical 'asceticism of the spirit'. The second stage, the 'time of the desert' ('like the camel that, burdened, speeds into the desert . . .' was to be pronounced by Zarathustra in setting the scene for the spirit's second metamorphosis), this second stage demands of the admiring heart that it should, even if it breaks, deny what it had admired most, gain freedom and independence by 'idealizing' what hitherto it had *not* loved and by attaching itself to 'contrary values', until, during the third stage, it learns boundlessly to 'affirm' and, knowing neither god nor man above itself, finally attains to that innocence of instinct ('the lion, finally, becomes a child', says Zarathustra) that is the condition of a new creativity.

'I took sides *against* myself and *for* everything that happened to hurt me . . .' It is indeed amazing how much of Nietzsche's own mind and autobiography is depicted in Zarathustra's evocation of the spirit in its 'camel' phase; and as far as its second metamorphosis is concerned, that 'lion', as is shown both by the preparatory note and the text of *Zarathustra*, was fated to become scarcely more than an even better camel in fulfilling the hardest and most self-hurting task of all—harder still than those for which the more modest animal needed 'heroic' strength.

'To humble oneself to wound one's pride'—he who has followed with fascination the eventful story, inscribed in his works and not only in his autobiographical utterances, of Nietzsche's relationship with Wagner, has good reason to believe that, looked upon not only from the vantage-point of *Zarathustra*, there *always* was an element of self-humiliation even in the most enthusiastic services the young author of *The Birth of Tragedy* and, more conspicuously, of *Richard Wagner in Bayreuth* had rendered the composer. It is certainly true to say that in *The Birth of Tragedy* Nietzsche, with his own profound metaphysical intuition and classical learning, indeed his genius, 'knelt down' before Wagner, just as if Dionysus and Apollo, the deities of the book, had come into their divine offices merely to pave the way for the musical return of Wotan. And is not that 'questionable' book—as Nietzsche himself called it eighteen years after he had written it[8]—flawed by its issuing, not too smoothly, into a kind of metaphysical advertisement for the composer-dramatist? And if it is a correct reading of some of Nietzsche's ecstatic dithyrambs to Dionysus to see in them his own—much delayed—love-songs for Cosima-Ariadne and indictments of Wagner-Theseus, then Tribschen, the place of Nietzsche's sojourns with Wagner and Cosima must have been to him the name for a labyrinthine state of the soul in which he was torn hither and thither by admiration, desire, jealousy, and self-effacement. Moreover, putting side by side his essay *Wagner in Bayreuth*, still aglow with the fervour of the apostle, and the most sceptical, indeed hostile notebook entries about Wagner that he wrote at the same time—observations that anticipate much of the anti-Wagner diatribe *The Wagner Case* (1888)—we may guess what Zarathustra means by the camel-spirit's mocking his secret wisdom through publicly letting his folly shine—in praise of a man whose unquestionable artistic powers he had even then come close to judging disastrous. And he *did* break with him at a time when Wagner had indeed triumphed and was no longer in need of Nietzsche's espousing his 'cause'. On the contrary, had he maintained his friendship, he might have shared a little of the light that now so abundantly shone upon Wagner, the very man of whom he said to Lou Salomé (in a letter written in the autumn of 1882 when *Parsifal* was performed for the first time in Bayreuth and Nietzsche, staying away from it, was in Tautenburg, not very far from the festival town) that he had '*erliebt*' his art (a word-play on '*erleben*'—to experience—and '*lieben*'—to love): 'It was altogether a long *passion*: I find no other word for it'; and then goes on to say that the break with Wagner was an act of renunciation which, although it was necessary if he was at last to find himself, was among the 'hardest and most melancholy things' he had ever experienced.

– 2 –

The sense of having climbed his 'high mountains' with the intent to challenge his enemy God—his hangman, as Zarathustra's magician calls him in one of Nietzsche's most sinister ventriloquisms,[9] his hangman, his agony, and yet his ultimate bliss—never quite left Nietzsche, as little as the feeling that he was 'tempting the tempter'. Indeed, the desire to do so is perhaps at the inmost core of his spiritual existence, the deepest secret of his psyche. Insofar as Thomas Mann's *Doctor Faustus* is a novel about Nietzsche, it is Nietzschean above all in presenting its hero, the composer Adrian Leverkühn, as the victim, both triumphant and tragic, of such 'tempting'; and surely Leverkühn might be found in the company of those men, most creative, lonely, and disturbed, into whose mouths Nietzsche put the words: 'Oh grant madness, you heavenly powers! Madness that at last I may believe in myself . . . I am consumed by doubts, for I have destroyed the Law . . . If I am not more than the Law, then I am the most abject of all men'.[10] For it was Leverkühn who had asked for the madness as well as the victorious self-assurance of genius, and was given both, although not by heavenly powers but by the Devil, the tempter whom he had tempted. The author of that prayer for madness, Nietzsche, had himself a perfect right to those words; and with even clearer autobiographical intent he once invented, alluding to the figure of the tempter's most notorious tempter, a character he called 'the Don Juan of the Mind' who, having been disillusioned by every attainable knowledge, found himself in the end seeking 'the knowledge which hurts most', and in the very end craved Hell itself, 'the only knowledge which can still seduce him'.[11] 1926468

Just as an unfathomable inner compulsion, both destructive and creative, made him 'send home', in his lived life, those who might have comforted his tortured soul—Lou Salomé, for instance, whom he loved, and allowed himself to be dominated by such 'friends' as his sister was, stone-deaf to the voice of his true mind, so was he driven, in his intellectual existence, to abandon every pasture that sustained his spiritual nature (the metaphysical domains, for instance, of *The Birth of Tragedy* and *Thoughts out of Season*) in order to feed, 'for the sake of the truth', 'on the acorns and grass of knowledge' that grew on the 'god-forsaken' fields of *Human, All-Too-Human*. But *was* it 'for the sake of the truth' that he wrote this antimetaphysical manifesto, the most brilliant and inspired document that nine-teenth-century positivism, indeed any form of positivism, has brought forth? To see it thus, would be seeing it too simply. For *Human, All-Too-Human*, his great experiment in spiritual defiance, is already pervaded by the sense of there being *no truth* whatever, and certainly no spiritual truth, and by the suspicion that what is called truth is merely 'the kind of error without which a certain type of animal finds it impossible to exist'.[12] Once this intuition and powerful agent within the intellectual sensibility, as productive of wittily tragic paradoxes as it is impotent in logic, has taken possession of a mind, the demand for intellectual honesty—the demand Nietzsche constantly and insistently made upon himself 'for the sake of the truth'—can only be met by irony, the kind of irony that looks like destiny rather than evasiveness, and with him often assumed the unironical appearance of extreme and extremely contradictory beliefs rehearsed simultaneously or in quick succession.

Where there is such a drought of truth, its waters will stagnate, and he who is none the less determined to step into them is likely to find himself in a morass, running after will-o'-the-wisps. 'Will-o'-the-wisps of the morasses' that 'simulate the stars': this is what Nietzsche, in the book that followed upon *Zarathustra*, in *Beyond Good and Evil*,[13] calls 'these great artists and altogether these higher beings'. All of them have, he writes, something to conceal in their souls, something terrible, 'some inner desecration', and 'lost in mud and almost in love with it', they rise from it, through the 'forgeries' of their works, to those heights of sublimity to which naïve and innocent spectators look up in pure adoration. Nietzsche, with his faculty to see great achievements as the compensatory manoeuvres of wounded and humiliated souls, may well have been what he once claimed he was: the first psychologist of Europe, one who would not be shy of 'frog or toad' or other creatures of the unclean waters if their habitats promised some 'truth'. But does intellectual honesty really demand that the seeker should seek the truth in muddy pools? A few pages after the swamp excursion, the author of *Beyond Good and Evil* is back on drier and cleaner ground: 'From which follows that it is the sign of a finer humanity to respect "the mask" and not, in the wrong places indulge in psychology and psychological curiosity'.[14] This is no longer spoken by the camel-spirit but by a mind who knows that 'truth' is not the sole criterion of Truth. And yet he speaks of masks. But where there is no true face, there can be no mask either, or else *only* masks. And psychology 'in the wrong places'? There are no wrong places where there is no right one. Or is the right place where, still in the vicinity of the 'morasses', we read the eminently psychological dictum: 'He who does not *wish* to see what is great in a man, has the sharpest eye for that which is low and superficial in him, and so gives away himself'?[15]

For every truth that departs from the world, there arrives a ghost. But there is one in particular whose acquaintance Nietzsche-Zarathustra has made, a demon-ghost who would frighten him and to whom he stretched out his hand in friendship as if it were the bearer of most joyful news. With this encounter ends the Fourth Book of *Cheerful Science*. It is that strange, beautiful, and still hesitant 'What if' rehearsal of the Eternal Recurrence, the idea which, together with the prophecy of the *Übermensch*, was to become the most resounding of

Zarathustra's messages. And as if to make quite sure that the connection between that passage and the prophetic book is not overlooked, it is followed, in *Cheerful Science*, by the beginning—anticipated there word for word—of *Thus Spoke Zarathustra*; word for word, but with an added heading: *'incipit tragoedia'*; and the tragic, catastrophic potential of the Eternal Recurrence does indeed emerge most clearly from the passage. It is entitled *'Das grösste Schwergewicht'* which may— but only just—be rendered as 'The greatest weight'; and what this translation loses of its original allusion to the integrating gravitational force, it gains by its closeness to the camel's heaviest burden. This is the text of 'The greatest weight':

What if one day or one night a demon secretly followed you into your loneliest solitude and said to you: 'This life, as you are living it now and have been living it, you will have to live once more and an infinite number of times; and nothing will be new in it, but every pain and every joy, and all that has been trivial in your life or great must be repeated, and all in the same sequence; and also this spider here and the moonlight between the trees; and also this moment and I myself. The eternal hourglass will be turned again and again— and you with it, you tiny grain of sand!' Would you throw yourself down and, gnashing your teeth, curse the demon who spoke thus? Or have you ever experienced a moment so tremendous that you would reply: 'You are a god and never have I heard anything more divine!' If that thought gained power over you, it would, as you are now, transform or perhaps crush you; the question: 'Do you want this once again and an infinite number of times?' would lie as the greatest weight upon everything you do. Or else: how deeply would you have to fall in love with yourself and with life in order not to desire anything more than this ultimate confirmation and seal.[16]

Nothing that Zarathustra will have to say later in announcing, with blatant conviction and without 'if' and 'when', the

Eternal Recurrence, will be as authentic as these poetic condi-
tionals, and nothing will be as translucent. Indeed, what shines
through this prose poem is the ground of tragic nihilism from
which the annunciation springs, the frightening 'or else' that
stipulates ecstasy as the sole condition in which existence may
be tolerable. For between the 'tremendous moment' that wills
itself again and again, and the cursing of the ghost, there stretches
nothing but gloomy nothingness. Therefore the author of 'The
greatest weight' cannot but suspect that no one except the
Übermensch would be able to press that seal of eternity upon
an existence that knows only time and time and time: time
and therefore only futility and death.

Certainly, Nietzsche, for himself, did not possess the power
to transform his time into this eternity. He who wrote: 'This
life—it is your life eternal'[17] confessed 'I do not wish to live
again', and added: 'How have I borne life? By creating. What
has made me endure? The vision of the *Übermensch* who affirms
life. I have tried to affirm life *myself*—but ah!'[18] And he said:
'I perform the great experiment: Who can bear the idea of the
Eternal Recurrence?—Those who cannot bear the sentence,
There is no salvation, *ought* to perish'.[19] This is how, in his
notebook and, as it were, behind the back of the reader of
Zarathustra, he explained why that demonic whisper of the
Eternal Recurrence would crush him who receives it in his
feeble nay-saying state. Or, even more frighteningly, he wrote:
'Let us consider this idea in its most terrible form: existence as
it is, without meaning or goal, but inescapably recurrent, without a finale into nothingness . . .'[20] And surely it is not by mere
accident that in the composition of *Cheerful Science* the passage
of 'The greatest weight' is preceded by Nietzsche's scintillating
reflection on the last words of Socrates; and 'scintillating' is the
mot juste if we consider the recklessly contradictory judgements

Nietzsche has passed on Socrates throughout his writings. Here Socrates is called brave and wise in everything he did, said, and did not say; serene, balanced, ironical, mischievous, amorous, and, above all, keeping discreetly silent on his ultimate knowledge. Yet his last words spoken before he drank the hemlock, 'ludicrous and terrifying' as they are, gave it away: 'Crito, I owe a cock to Asclepius'; and, Nietzsche writes, he who understands them aright suddenly discovers that Socrates, who had lived in public like a soldier of truth, was surreptitiously a pessimist who was sick of life, looking upon it as a disease and upon death as the cure. (The sick of Athens who appealed to the spirit of the great healer Asclepius for recovery used to offer him a cock in sacrifice.) Whereupon follows Nietzsche's final injunction: 'Friends, we must overcome even the Greeks!' And this overcoming was to be accomplished by means of that total affirmation of individual existence demanded by the demon's message of the Eternal Recurrence.

What Nietzsche here says of Socrates is, of course, at the same time yet another fragment from his autobiography: 'I do not wish to live *again*.' For such a man, to pronounce a Yea-saying as all-embracing, extreme, and fanatical as is contained in the doctrine of the Eternal Recurrence, is indeed to 'take sides *against*' himself and '*for* anything that happened to hurt and was hard' for him; is 'to offer a hand to the ghost' that terrified him. 'All these most difficult things the spirit that would bear much takes upon itself: like the camel that, burdened, speeds into the desert, thus the spirit speeds into its desert.' And here, in its 'loneliest desert', the 'second metamorphosis occurs': 'the spirit becomes a lion who would win his freedom and be master in its own desert.' The external scene, be it noted, remains a desert, and we have already ventured to say that, in a sense, the lion too remains a camel.

It still carries a heavy burden: life. But in his soul he has accepted it so profoundly that what had been oppression has become lightness and feline grace, the 'greatest weight' has turned into weightlessness, and the enslavement of the humble creature into the freedom of the unburdened lion who

seeks out his last master: he wants to fight him and his last god; for ultimate victory he wants to fight with the great dragon.

Who is the great dragon whom the spirit will no longer call lord and god? 'Thou shalt' is the name of the great dragon. But the spirit of the lion says, 'I will'. 'Thou shalt' lies in his way, sparkling like gold, an animal covered with scales; and on every scale shines a golden 'thou shalt'.

Values, thousands of years old, shine on those scales; and thus speaks the mightiest of dragons: 'All value of all things shine on me. All value has long been created, and I am all created value. Verily, there shall be no more "I will".' Thus speaks the dragon.

My brothers, why is there a need in the spirit for the lion? Why is not the beast of burden, which renounces and is reverent, enough?[21]

The idiom is more garish and luxuriant than befits a desert, the pseudo-biblical tone is as unbearable as the camel's burden, and the Wagnerian dragon is only waiting, with alarming obviousness, for a Siegfried to kill him. Yet the meaning is clear, too clear to be much upset by its allegorical ornamentations: There is no moral law and therefore no moral duty. Dead is the old god from whom once issued both the law and the duty, and who was, in fact or rather in allegory, the maker of all the dragon's scales with their 'Thou shalts'. What, therefore, is needed, is new tables, new values. To create them, so Nietzsche's parable continues, does not lie within the province of the lion. Certainly, it is not exactly a constructive animal; it may build lairs for itself, but no Mount Sinais for mankind. But what it can do—to stay within the terms of the anti-moral fable—is to conquer the sphere of freedom that the spirit needs for a new creativity. The first step towards such freedom is 'a sacred No' where the camel had nodded its profane assent: in the face of Duty that now issues from nowhere, and of the unending 'Thou shalt' that has been deprived of its lawgiver. This at least is within the power of the beast of prey.

Here again, Zarathustra's first speech has succeeded, if in nothing else, at least in abbreviating, to the point of its appearing simple-minded, a long, complex, and tragic story. Its focal theme is: What is the nature of morality? Nietzsche, whose whole spiritual existence was dominated by this question, wrestled with it again and again—after the time of *Zarathustra* specifically in *Beyond Good and Evil* and *The Genealogy of Morals*—and failed. It is overwhelmingly true to say that this was a failure distinguished from most failures by the intellectual passion that went into the pursuit of the elusive goal—such passion as always, it would seem, is only another name for failures of grand dimensions. And has not the enterprise produced most brilliant insights? And does it not give the impression that it has been undertaken on the prompting of historical necessity itself? And yet . . .

While Nietzsche, with regard to a *certain* moral tradition, the Christian, his own, was eminently perceptive in registering its decadence and thus its waning authenticity, its lagging vitality and thus its spiritual obstructiveness, its lack of genuine conviction and thus its culturally enfeebling effect; and while, goaded on by his spiritual discontent, he was inexhaustibly ingenious in analysing the psychology of the Christian 'camel-spirit': the pleasure it takes in carrying the burden of its cross, the excitements it experiences in ascetic renunciation, the erotic delights it finds in degrading Eros from a divine being to a vice, the sensation of power it enjoys in extolling the virtues of powerlessness and humility and thus afflicting the naïvely strong with a sense of guilt; while he excelled in ever subtler and, towards the end, ever louder and more percussive variations on these themes, he left the question behind the themes untouched and unanswered: What is the meaning of the compulsion, deeply rooted in human beings and probably in being human, to make moral distinctions and to know good from evil—so that no 'evil' is morally acceptable to man, no infamy, no deceit, no shamelessness, no hatred, without his 'revaluing' it as good. If there is anything that deserves to be called 'human nature', then it is moral in the sense that it is unthinkable without the faculty, indeed the innate need, of discriminating morally (and aesthetic judgements are, in their structure, so close to moral ones that sometimes they become indistinguishable from them). Even the great Christian injunction 'Judge not, that ye be not judged' makes a moral judgement in condemning self-righteousness, and threatens the soul with the judge it will have to face eventually; and Nietzsche's vision of a sphere 'beyond good and evil' is radiant with his hope of a radically new goodness. This is what he never quite acknowledged. Mostly he spoke like a physician who, diagnosing the harm done by a commonly indulged unwholesome diet, ignores the inescapable need for nourishment.

Or did he? Not quite when, for instance, he made his Zarathustra speak of the 'creation of new values', values not in the slightest 'a-moral' (there are no such values) but only different, *morally*, from those of the Christian inheritance; and certainly not at all when his prophet prophesies the this hybrid of vision and contrivance, is, by implication, *Übermensch*. For this paragon of a new and higher humanity, this hybrid of vision and contrivance, is, by implication Nietzsche's acknowledgement of the death of man, bound to occur in the wake of the notorious death of God; and the strange cause of the human demise is that 'absurdity' of man's nature which Nietzsche, although he was neither its discoverer nor inventor (within the Christian tradition he is, to be sure, preceded by Pascal and Kierkegaard), has yet explored and analysed with obsessive persistence, intuition, and ingenuity. That 'absurd' state of affairs lies in the incompatibility, dramatized by the death of God, of the spiritual and moral needs of man and the character of the world into which he has come. Endowed with an insatiable appetite for 'meaning', he is helplessly caught in the meaningless machinery of existence; ever anxious to justify his manner of living, he finds himself in a life devoid of judge or sanction; and desiring to make a little sense of his having been born and his having to die, he receives no sign or signal from the vast surrounding senselessness.

It is this absurd consciousness which after the death of God is both incurable and intolerable. Nietzsche looks upon it as the sensibility of nihilism, the condition of mind and soul which, for a while, will still be just supportable by means of the spiritual pittance left over from the past, but is bound to end catastrophically. For the ground gives, and 'the wasteland grows' and 'soon, where we live, nobody will be able to exist'.[22] Nobody, that is, before man's final metamorphosis into the *Übermensch* who, without being a god, will no longer be merely human; for he will have overcome the great nihilistic malaise, will have risen above the doom of absurdity, will, without going out in search for the waters of truth, strike the water of life itself from the dry sands of the desert, will lead the good life without needing the unattainable knowledge of the good, and will exist in glory without having to borrow it from that God who once let his light shine upon man and now is no more. Yet to come into this resplendent fortune, he will have to be more, unthinkably more, than the lion of Zarathustra's first speech and parable; for 'to create new values—that even the lion cannot do'. To do this, the spirit will have to be as a child. 'Except ye . . . become like little children, ye shall not enter into the kingdom of heaven.' Is it possible that Zarathustra speaks here with the voice of St Matthew? It is; and here, amid all the biblical pastiche in which the book abounds, its speech touches with a measure of authenticity upon the biblical theme of grace:

But . . . what can the child do that even the lion could not do? Why must the preying lion still become a child? The child is innocence and forgetting, a new beginning, a game, a self-propelled wheel, a first movement, a sacred Yes. For the game of creation . . . a sacred Yes is needed: the spirit now wills his own will and he who had been lost to the world now conquers his own world.[23]

This is how Zarathustra speaks of the lion's finally becoming a child. Even some ten years earlier—at that time Nietzsche was Professor of Classical Philology in Basel—he had spoken to his students, in a very unprofessorial and poetically self-willed interpretation of Heraclitus, of the child at play. There it served as the model image of the original force that has brought forth the world by playing its creator-game 'in eternally unruffled innocence' and to no purpose other than the pleasure afforded by the pure aesthetic contemplation of the playfully created things.[24] In *The Birth of Tragedy*, written just before, it was this beholding of life as a pure 'aesthetic phenomenon' that was the only 'eternal justification' of the world.[25] But now it is lion into child, the parabolic and utopian definition of the *Übermensch*.

– 3 –

The problem involved defies every attempt to confine it

historically. For it begins, if ever it began, far back in mythic time: with the parting of the human mind from Mind, from the domain of Plato's Ideas, and with its descent into the darkness that was to be only dimly illuminated by what little transpired of the Ideas' light. Man, from then on, has had merely a vague idea of himself and not, alas, his Reality. He has felt ill at ease ever since. Or in a different idiom, in the language of Genesis: the curse fell upon him with his eating from the Tree of Knowledge, the curse that was believed, by St Matthew and the other evangelists of salvation, to be removable only through the faith that is the child's. Without this faith there is only the affliction of self-consciousness, the grown man's shame and embarrassment at being his naked separate self, the particular punishment within the universal punishment that is called the Fall. Yet as long as God was, there was the hope of redemption. It was only when the malady came which, in Nietzsche's diagnosis, originated in the death of God, that human minds applied themselves to the huge task of designing a *historical* future in terms of paradise regained: this would come about with the overcoming of self-consciousness and with the recovery, or a new creation, of innocence and naïve spontaneity. When Rousseau demanded man's return to Nature, he meant such an Eden; and Hegel, who saw the 'unhappy consciousness' plunged into sadness at every turn of its way by the ever-repeated discovery that 'objective reality' was unyieldingly made of stuff different from Spirit, believed that finally the Real would be so profusely irradiated by Mind, indeed transformed into it, that the suffering of consciousness would end in the final consummation of its oneness with the world, indeed its *being* the world. (It was this secular messianism of Hegel's that Marx turned around from mind, 'the head', on to the material 'feet' of the classless society, a society without contradictions and no longer offensive to the true mind of humanity.)

Endless and endlessly varied are the configurations of thought and vision produced by the intermingling of Rousseau's 'Back to Nature' and Hegel's 'Forward to Mind'; but what all have in common is the longing for, indeed the expectation of, a state of being in which self-consciousness, the persistent obstacle in the soul's reaching out for its freedom, is done away with and dissolved in that 'naïveté' and 'innocence' at last restored or attained. This restoration or attainment would be distinguished by the identity of what *is* and what *seems*, of *being* and *doing*, that identity of which Nature is the constant reminder and 'the Child' the promise. In his great essay 'On Naive and Reflective Poetry', Schiller says of all things in Nature that they *are* what we *were* (again, as with Rousseau, the lost paradise of the natural state), but also what we ought to become by way of reason and freedom (again, as with Hegel, the natural undistracted rule of freedom and reason, paradise regained). This is why Nature 'represents our lost childhood ... and thus fills us with a certain melancholy' (for childhood is the only remnant of 'unmutilated nature' to be met with in our civilized condition), but, in providing us at the same time with 'the ideal of our highest perfection', also 'sublimely elates us'.[26]

It is this 'sense sublime', the philosophy of the child's pure and unselfconscious being, the Heaven which 'lies about us in our infancy', that Wordsworth celebrates in 'Intimations of Immortality', and to which Kleist has devoted his beautiful philosophical dialogue 'On the Marionette Theatre' where a dancer, a ballet master, in seeking out the perfect model of graceful movement, goes back beyond the child, even beyond the sphere of organic nature, to the mechanical contraption of the marionette; for in its absolute and unconscious obedience to natural laws, the laws of weight and counterweight, the marionette displays in its motions a grace that is wholly *unaffected*—unaffected, that is, by even the slightest trace of self-consciousness, a grace that is not attainable by any man or woman: 'Only a god could, in this respect, be its equal.' Only a god, the child-god; this, adds the dancer, is the point where in our circular world the two extremes meet: the unconscious and the perfect consciousness. And as his partner responds with incredulous surprise to this lesson, he asks him whether he had ever read with attentiveness the third chapter of Genesis: only he who has grasped the meaning of this beginning of human history, will be able intelligently to speak of its end: '. . . that we shall have to eat once again from the Tree of Knowledge to fall back into the state of innocence'—the state of grace that an infinite consciousness would share with the unconscious marionette, or with the children of paradise before the serpent led them into temptation, shame, and the awareness of their selfhood.

Kleist's dialogue on the marionettes has supplied the theatrical as well as the intellectual scenery of the most elegiac of Rilke's *Duino Elegies*, the fourth, where the stage—the stage of human inwardness—is set for the farewell enacted before the backdrop of the 'well-known garden'; and there appears that dancer whom the spectator-poet angrily rejects: 'No, not *this* one!' For however hard he tries to posture with grace and lightness, he is heavy with the consciousness of *not being* what he *acts*. He is nothing but a bourgeois in disguise, will soon remove his make-up and go home, 'entering by the kitchen': 'I do not want these half-filled masks. Let puppets dance! They at least are undivided.' But the ultimate and at last *real* show will be enacted only when the Angel—Rilke's embodiment of 'the fullness of being'—will hold in his hands the wires of the puppet.

'Angel and puppet!'—only then will the seasons of our lives add up to the unbroken circle, to that integrity of existence of which childhood is the foreshadowing. The Fourth Elegy is Rilke's version of the last act played on Kleist's Marionette Theatre and the elegiac celebration of Nietzsche's Child-Übermensch.

What Kleist and Rilke personified in the bad dancer, Nietzsche again and again spoke of as 'the problem of the *actor*': 'the "dissembling", the typical ability to transform himself' was 'a flaw in his character', as a jotting from the year 1888 disjointedly puts it.[27] But it was, of course, not only, indeed not at all, the professional actor that fascinated him; and not only the artist's consciously held and cultivated idea that he *is* an artist and has to conduct himself like one—a fact of the modern artistic consciousness that for Schiller made modern art 'sentimental' (the word used in his particular sense, meaning 'reflective' or 'self-conscious'); that for Hegel signalled 'the end of art'; and for Nietzsche made some art, for instance and above all the art of Richard Wagner, into a variant of the actor's craft.[28] No, what haunted Nietzsche in his later years like a malevolent ghost was the pervasive suspicion that the self-consciousness of the intelligence had grown to such a degree as to deprive *any* belief of its genuineness: to believe is now a form of self-deception, and to expound a conviction has become unthinkable without an ingredient of that rhetorical dishonesty that Zarathustra, equating it with lying, calls poetry, the poetry of poets and his own.[29] When madness had overtaken Nietzsche, he wrote (6 January 1889) that fantastic and uncannily revealing letter to Jacob Burckhardt, the professor of history in Basel, in which he, the self-retired professor of classical philology from the same university, ironically and madly confessed that he too would have preferred to retain his Chair to having to be God, a god, moreover, who was condemned 'to entertain the next eternity with bad witticisms'. This is the last time that Nietzsche speaks of that 'buffoonery', the 'mask of despair', which had become his persistent characterization of much in the intellectual, artistic, and religious life of modernity—and insanely applies it to himself.

Twice in his notebooks he asked why everything in this civilization ends as a kind of histrionic display, as 'acting'; and twice he states, by way of answering his own question, that insofar as anything is the product of the conscious will, it must needs lack perfection;[30] for everything that *is* perfect has at all times resulted from 'the automatism', as he called it in his *Anti-Christ*,[31] of a deep and sure instinct. Such instinct is not to be found any more among modern men. Zarathustra's consciously willed *leonitas* must therefore fail in creating the new values of a new humanity. Within a world intellectually articulated by Nietzsche, the *Duino Elegies*, Transcendental Idealism or the Romantic expectation—in such a world can the Spirit ever succeed in accomplishing its third and final metamorphosis and become the child that, playing in self-forgetfulness, will give us the new law? Or must not the last word be the terrible prayer for that madness in which the prophet may at last believe in himself and his prophecy? If hesitatingly we begin to essay an answer, it will perhaps lie in a consciousness that, even if it does not create out of itself a new unselfconscious spontaneity, is at least imbued with something that in less self-conscious times was called goodness, and may still be acceptable under the name of sympathy, a sympathy certainly not to be withheld from Nietzsche despite the excesses indulged by his mind. For he was a man in whom the self and the poem, the thinker and the thought, are as much at one as are his loneliness and his world, his suffering and his genius.

III

Rilke in Paris

On 20 June 1907 Rilke wrote from Paris that, as so often before, he had—not without scruples—defencelessly surrendered to that great and inexorable city, new to him whenever he returned to it, fatal to him in all its charm.[1] Only a month before, he had left Capri where the hospitable Villa Discopoli had housed him, and already Paris had made the island appear 'far off', unreal in its sheltered dreaminess. And in another letter written on the same day he spoke of the jealous nature of Paris that seemed to refuse sharing him with anything else in the world. Paris: it was for him more a man-made landscape than a town; for the heavens, he wrote, 'form a canopy over this city . . . as they do over the sea'.[2] If now it was hard for him to hold his unsure ground against the overwhelming 'reality' of Paris, there must have been moments at least when Capri too assailed him most vigorously: Capri's nocturnal sky, for instance, in that night the memory of which is preserved in his 'Song of the Sea'. 'Capri-Piccola marina' is written under the title as the poem's geographical definition, and end of January 1907 is the time he wrote it:

> wenn einer wacht,
> so muss er sehn, wie er
> dich übersteht:
>   uraltes Wehn vom Meer,
> welches weht
> nur wie für Ur-Gestein,
> lauter Raum
> reissend von weit herein . . .

In a prose paraphrase: Let him who is awake in such a night find a way of withstanding the ageless rush of the wind from the sea, the turbulent air that seems to be meant for primeval rock rather than human beings, as it tears along with it nothing but space from afar. And further on: Up there the fig tree, rising into the light of the moon, understands perhaps the storm's intimation.

It is the first of the poems collected in *Der neuen Gedichte anderer Teil* (1908), the second part of *Neue Gedichte* (*New Poems*, 1907–8), the first poem in the order of writing, that is, not in the printed sequence. It is exquisite, and made an 'unforgettable' and 'indescribable' impression, when according to the memoir of the great maternal friend of his later years, Princess Marie von Thurn und Taxis-Hohenlohe, he read it out one evening in the castle of Duino with the darkening Adriatic stretching outside the window. His two listeners were his hostess, the Princess, and her other guest, the philosopher Rudolf Kassner to whom ten years later the eighth of the *Duino Elegies* was to be dedicated. This reading took place in April 1912 and the brief 'Song of the Sea' was, as it were, a mere encore. For the *première* was Rilke's reciting the first two of the *Duino Elegies*. He had completed them only a few months before when he resided in the castle all by himself. For the two preceding years he had suffered what he took to be the drying-up of the springs of poetry. In his hopelessness he feared that this was to be his permanent condition after he had attempted to rid himself of his misery by making Malte Laurids Brigge miserable, the hero of his one novel—if it is a novel and not rather what the title says it is: *The Notebooks of Malte Laurids Brigge*, the work that he wrote in fits and starts between 1902 and 1910, years dominated, like the book, by Paris, the city that was also the exile of his literary double, the young Danish poet Malte. Instead of liberating Rilke, the writing of the book added exhaustion to despair, although immediately after its completion he wrote to Anton Kippenberg that, having gone through Malte's agonies, it would be possible for him to write any amount of poetry.[3] Of course, he must have known that Kippenberg, his patient publisher and friend, was waiting for such a hopeful message. Still, for the time being the hope proved illusory. Once the book was published in 1910, he uttered time and again the anxious conviction that this record of an indomitable fear—the 'existential' fear which decades later was to become the password to literary respectability on the Boulevard St Germain—would remain the conclusion and melancholy testament of his life. But then the miracle of Duino came to pass, sudden, unannounced and effortless. The story has been told so often that it hardly bears repetition: how in the morning he had received a tiresome business letter; how he immersed himself in figures and legal arguments; how after some hours he interrupted the unwelcome labour of composing a reply and walked up and down the path that led along the bastions of the castle where there is a steep drop of cliffs into the sea; and how out of the strong wind, the Bora, a voice broke into his prosaic deliberations and spoke the words that are the beginning of the *Duino Elegies*:

> Wer, wenn ich schriee, hörte mich denn aus der Engel Ordnungen?

(Who, if I cried, would even hear me in the order of Angels?); and how, upon returning to his room with the precious dictate, he not only finished the difficult letter but also, within a few hours, the whole of the First Elegy, while the Second, the truly angelic one, followed suit within a short time. But at this point the overwhelming inspiration ceased and would not come back with sufficient strength to bring one of the greatest poetic designs to completion—not, that is, until ten years later, in 1922, when in the haunted tower, known to the inhabitants of the beautiful upper Rhône valley as the Castle Muzot, the poet finished, as if in a fever, the whole cycle of the elegies. Within the same few February weeks he also wrote the *Sonnets to Orpheus*. As he jubilantly announced to Princess Marie his deliverance from years of apprehension—'But now *it is*. *IS*, Amen. So I've survived up to this, . . . through it all . . . And it was this that was needed. *Only* this . . . ',[4] he also said that the *Elegies* belonged to her: instead of a dedication they would bear the inscription 'The property of Princess Marie von Thurn und Taxis-Hohenlohe'. For it was her castle, 'towering into sky and sea', 'a promontory of human existence', as he called it in a letter of October 1911,[5] where the voice spoke for the first time and where on that April evening of 1912 he recited the first two Elegies, adding the 'Song of the Sea'. The song was written five years earlier, soon after he had gone back to Capri from Naples where he had spent a few days with his wife, the sculptor and painter Clara Westhoff.

It was one of those matrimonial reunions, happy, it seems, because they were brief, that had become the rule and condition of their married life. His diary of those Naples days reports that they visited the Museo Nazionale to see again the Greek funeral relief of Orpheus, Eurydice, and Hermes, that in 1904 had inspired him to write his long narrative poem on masculine restlessness, feminine repose, on passion, farewell and death, so successful a poem on Rilke's very own themes and preoccupations that one may suspect he would have invented the story of Orpheus had it not come to him from antiquity; and the stele makes yet another appearance in his poetry: at the very conclusion of that Second Elegy, that was also the end of the Duino epiphany:

On Attic steles, did not the circumspection
of human gesture amaze you? Were not love and farewell
so lightly laid upon shoulders, they seemed to be made
of other stuff than with us? Remember the hands,
how they rest without pressure, though power is there in the
torsos.
The wisdom of those self-masters was this: so far it is our
domain,
ours is to touch one another like this; beyond it,
more strongly, the gods press upon us; but that is the
gods' affair.
. . .
                                    . . . True, our heart
transcends us
just as it did the Greeks. But we can no longer
gaze after it into figures that soothe it, or godlike
bodies that in their grandeur restrain it.*

The Naples diary of those days also tells of a visit to the Certosa.
There the two gazed into the depth of a well, vainly trying to
separate what could be seen in the water—the mirror image of
clouds and at the bottom of the well green weeds—from the
reflection of their own faces; and Rilke quotes Clara as saying:
'This is how it always is in life: It is impossible to see anything
without ourselves getting into the picture.'[6]

Did she know then that this casual observation was all but the
formula of the poet's struggles with the genius of his poetry, of
those conflagrations of soul and mind that more than any external events are Rilke's biography during the Paris years; and Paris
years they are, the years from 1902 to the outbreak of the First

---

* The translations of passages from *Duino Elegies* here and elsewhere are
taken from their English rendering by J. B. Leishman and Stephen Spender
(London 1939), but I modified some lines in order to obtain the particular
emphasis required by my context.

World War in 1914. It is not for nothing that Paris is the scene
of the central Fifth Elegy, Paris, the '*unendlicher Schauplatz*',
the 'infinite show-place'. To be sure, the locale of our episodes
is Capri or Naples or Duino; and many are the poet's short or
extended sojourns during those years in practically every
continental country. Yet Paris would reclaim him after each of
his attempts to escape or to seek relief from his persistent
financial straits in the generous and often palatial offerings of
hospitality coming to him with a kind of fidgety regularity
from places as far apart as Scandinavia and the south of Italy,
not to mention the many appointments as travel companion
that took him, among other destinations, to Russia and Egypt.
Very much like Nietzsche, his unhappy predecessor in seeking
the love of Lou Salomé, the beautiful, soulful, intelligent and,
it would seem, not a little predatory *fin de siècle* lady from
Russia, Rilke was addicted to the belief that he had Slav blood
in his veins; and he liked to ascribe it to this inheritance that
the Russian journeys he undertook in the company of Lou in
1899 and 1900 (the year of Nietzsche's death) made him
discover his true spiritual home. But this was a poetic invention,
most clearly shown, perhaps, by his rapturous praise of Drojin,
the not very remarkable peasant-poet, or by the epistolary trans-
formation of his pilgrimage to Tolstoy's Yasnaya Polyana, which
was a *débâcle*, into a profound experience of the spirit. No,
despite his two visits, Russia remained a dream. The reality was
Paris, and Paris would not let go. Each time he returned to it
it was a home-coming: he was in his element; or rather in his
state of complex ambivalence, contentedly resuming his walks
through the Jardin du Luxembourg with its children, govern-
esses, lovers, or sometimes, strolling performers and acrobats,
and at the same time venting in letter after letter his exasperation
at the senseless, noisy bustle of the city that reeked of poverty,

sickness and death, and where 'the modiste Madame Lamort'

> winds and binds the restless ways of the world,
> those endless ribbons, . . .
>
> . . .
>
> all falsely coloured, to deck
> the cheap winter-hats of Fate,

as can be read in the Fifth Elegy, or in the words of the opening
sentence of *Malte Laurids Brigge*, that are preceded, like a letter,
by Rilke's own first Parisian address rue Toullier in the district
of the hospitals: 'So, then, people do come here in order to live;
I would sooner have thought one died here.'[7] Yet when in the
autumn of 1920, after the long interruption of the war, he was
in Paris again, this is what he wrote: ' . . . everything is absol-
utely right; for the first time since the dreadful years I am feeling
the continuity of my existence . . .' For here at last it was again:
the same richness of life, the same intensity, the same rightness
even in all the bad things.[8] But only a few months before the
outbreak of the war that inflicted on him the long separation
from the city, he had announced to the Princess that he was
'sick to death of Paris; it is a city of the damned'. He added that
he always knew this, but in the old days an angel told him the
meaning of his and their torments; now that the angel had
fallen silent, the misery was only petty and mean. Ambivalence,
indeed!

What *was* the angel's interpretation of the wretched plight?
Was it perhaps what Malte said of a writer he admired (he
meant, without naming him, Ibsen)? Created, as this writer was,
in the mould of a 'timeless tragic poet', he yet lived in an age
that would not easily supply the common signs and outward
gestures needed to make a great drama, but forced the poet ever
deeper into the recesses of subjectivity. Therefore he, the born

dramatist, had to search, impatiently, desperately, among
visible things and actions for what might still serve on the stage
of the world as the external equivalent of the inner vision, and
succeeded only through what Malte calls 'unexampled acts
of violence', deeds that forced the symbol-bound flights of the
imagination into the stuffy rooms and kitchens of the passers-
by whom Ibsen observed from his window and in the end
did nothing else in stubborn apathy. Well, yes, there was a
wild duck in a cage, 'a room where someone paces to and fro,
there was a clatter of glass in the next room, a fire outside the
window, there was the sun . . . But that was not enough.'[9]
What Rilke meant in speaking of Ibsen's search was exactly
what ten years later T. S. Eliot called the 'objective correlative'
of the inner emotion.[10]

This, then, may well have been one of the causes of Rilke's
helpless attachment to Paris: that it proved to him in the most
colourful and spectacular manner that severance between
within and without. There was the magnificence of the
churches that enveloped spaces deserted by God; there were the
grandiose designs of palaces and boulevards long since deprived
of the reality of power; or, to think again of the most Parisian
of the *Elegies*, the fifth, the showmen and acrobats whose
virtuosity fed upon, indeed consumed, all inner resources.
(It is not for nothing that the acrobats, the dancers, the circus
artists, all those 'unreal' beings that have learned to *do* so very
much more than they *are*, became one of the fascinations of
that period's art: Manet, Toulouse-Lautrec, Picasso, Rilke,
Kafka, Thomas Mann.) Thus, Paris drove Rilke relentlessly on
in his quest for the place—'where, o where is the place?', is the
questioning exclamation of the Fifth Elegy—where outward
expression and inner substance, word and meaning come together again. As it is now, Malte, that is, Rilke, still writes down

this and that, but 'there will come a day when my hand will be far from me; and bidding it write, I shall make it write words I do not mean. The time . . . is near, when not one word will remain upon another, and all meaning will dissolve like clouds and fall down like rain'.[11] This is a variation on a text by Hofmannsthal: his fictitious young Lord Chandos explaining to his protector, Francis Bacon, why he cannot write poetry any more. But whereas Hofmannsthal all but ceased to be a lyrical poet after the Chandos Letter (August 1902), Rilke— perhaps through 'acts of unexampled violence'—lived through that crescendo of anxieties that fills one of the best pages of *Malte Laurids Brigge* and ends with the *Angst* that 'I may give myself away and tell all that I dread; and the fear that I might not be able to say anything, because everything is unsayable,—and the other fears, . . . the fears'.[12] Yet Rilke lived through them and turned the unsayable into most remarkable poetry.

The documents of Rilke's Paris existence are *Malte Laurids Brigge*, *New Poems* of 1907 and 1908, and the beginning of the *Duino Elegies*, this ultimate, most 'violent' onslaught and perhaps conquest of the poetic and more than poetic unhappiness the scene and symbol of which is Paris. It is no great exaggeration to say that these three works comprise Rilke's biography of the decade in question. Of course, there were travels, flirtations, conversations, and those letters, letters, letters, which are endlessly protracted signals from the exposed and forever endangered borderland between 'life' and art, a demimonde where often even the demonstrably genuine takes on the appearance of the false, and the most determined seriousness seems to be given the lie by the sustained, gentle, often unendurable grimacing of the style (and alas, this epistolary manner again and again spills over on to the pages of *Malte Laurids Brigge*, rendering

some unreadable or at least, with their *Jugendstil* ornamentations, embarrassing in the extreme). There was also during the
later Paris years, Marthe, the remarkable and somewhat mysterious waif, the child lover, an inordinately unruly daughter
and a most charming lover whom he truly loved (if ever there
could be true love for one who said of himself that loving and
being loved were destined to count for nothing in his ultimate
dedication to solitude and poetry.)[13] And, yes, there was Clara,
his wife; and there was, towering above everything else, Rodin,
Clara's one-time teacher and Rilke's friend and for some months
even his employer (the poet was his secretary in 1905–6), the
irascible artist whose fits of rage made for rather tempestuous
and impermanent relationships. Rilke behaved nobly throughout the storms and dedicated the second part of *Neue Gedichte*
'À mon grand ami Auguste Rodin' (although this, given their
relative fames at the time and Rodin's lack of German, may
have been a dedication not quite free of boastfulness). But to
mention Rodin—and later the paintings of Cézanne—is to step
right back from 'life' into art, or rather to enter again those
regions of Rilke's biography that are written into his poetry.

Neue Gedichte (*New Poems*) are distinguished from anything
Rilke had written before by the particular determination to
grasp hold of the very essence of whatever may be the subject-
matter of the individual poem: a Buddha, a merry-go-round,
Christ in the Garden of Olives, a unicorn, a Roman sarcophagus,
a panther, a cathedral, laces, a blue or pink hydrangea, the
trinity of Orpheus, Eurydice, and Hermes, an archaic torso of
Apollo, Venice in the late autumn, flamingos, or that wind from
the sea which, although the song commemorates the nocturnal
Piccola Marina of Capri, does, as it were, blow from Paris,
tearing along with it not only empty space from afar but also
severing, after the manner of the hypnotically grand and terri-

fying city, the link that binds the soul of man to the world surrounding him. Like no other poem in the cycle, 'The Song of the Sea' not only *is* the scene it evokes but also states the condition of the poetic theory, both simple and amazing, that underlies *Neue Gedichte*, their 'thingness', their character as *'Ding-Gedichte'*, 'thing-poems', the poet's insistence, that is, upon the impossible: that they should present 'the things in and for themselves', avoiding even the slightest trace of what Ruskin called the 'pathetic fallacy', the projection of human emotions, passions, moods, desires, imaginings—in short: subjectivity—into the evocation of things. Why? Because we have become, if we not always were, outcasts, illegitimate inhabitants of the world, creatures who, as the First Elegy will have it, are by no means securely at home in the inherited interpretations of our existence: 'Is it possible that the whole history of the world has been misunderstood?', is the question asked by Malte Laurids Brigge; and his answer is: 'Yes, it is possible.'[14] Nothing here and now and beyond is prepared to receive our confidences, or intimate to us its meaning. Therefore, the ageless rush of the wind from the sea is not meant for us—'*du kommst zu keinem her*'—has no message whatsoever for us as it whirls around the ancient rocks and bends and sways the fig tree to its will.

The Romantic dream has ended with a rude awakening. If Goethe was still able to write the kind of poetry in which Nature was the *postillon d'amour* delivering news from the outside world at the address of the human soul and at the same time receiving the heart's acknowledgements, Rilke—the Rilke of Paris, the Rilke of *Neue Gedichte*—believes that he must divest himself of his self and sink it into 'the things', just as once upon a time the mystics immersed and lost themselves in the entirely other Being of God. By an oversight of literary history

Rilke was not personally acquainted with Proust, his closest spiritual relation and, like him, a transcendental snob; but he greatly admired what he knew of his work and sent to the Princess the first volume of *À la recherche du temps perdu* in the very year of its first publication: 1913. Did he recognize that the opening page of *Swann's Way* contains a description of the narrator's sensibility that bestowed upon him as a free gift what Rilke in his early thirties strove to achieve in the poetry of the 'thing poems' of *Neue Gedichte*: the total absorption of the poet's self in the object of his contemplation. For the 'I' of Proust's novel reports that after the first moments of sleep, he would wake up again into a state of consciousness that was half dream, half wakefulness; and in this condition it would seem to him that he had become what he had read about before falling asleep: 'a church, a quartet, the rivalry between François I and Charles V'. It was no doubt the poetico-mystical exercises of many years that made Rilke in the end susceptible to the same fits of lost identity: in 1914 he wrote to Lou Salomé that he felt so hopelessly unstable in his own being that he would fall a prey to every outside disturbance: ' . . . if there is a noise somewhere, . . . then I am that noise.'[15] Or has this not perhaps been the modern lyrical condition ever since Keats lamented the loss of 'identical self' suffered by the poet,[16] and since Goethe spoke of the 'umbilical cord' that, uncut throughout his life, bound him to Nature herself, preventing him—Goethe!— from being a sharply contoured individual but condemned him to the state of an oyster in the ocean over which pass mysterious waves;[17] and once, in his *Torquato Tasso*, he even compared the poet to a silkworm spinning himself into the cocoon as if into his coffin.

If Rilke is merely a latecomer in this pilgrimage towards poetic self-lessness, he has added not merely a new episode to

its history but given it a new quality: he raised this poetic fate
to the level of an aesthetic philosophy, a conscious method, that
he expressed nowhere more firmly than in the 'Requiem' he
wrote in the autumn of 1908 in Paris. It mourns a young man,
Wolf Graf von Kalckreuth who, at nineteen, had put an end
to his life because of an unhappy love. He had made attempts
at writing poetry, and it is this that provided Rilke with the
pretext for stating his idea of the 'thing-poem' with a precision
never before achieved. The unhappy young man might have
been saved, Rilke believes, had he endured as a poet, a poet,
that is, who would have learned the lesson that the maker of
the 'thing-poems' could have taught him, one who had out-
grown the Romantic belief that poetry is the proper vehicle for
communicating personal emotions, be they sad or joyful. Such
poets, Rilke writes, are like invalids employing language in
order to say where it hurts, instead of using words for building
an edifice of poetry after the manner of medieval stone-masons
who sank their selves into the equanimity of stone. For it is
the poet's destiny itself that enters into his verse, never to
return, or rather, it is his true destiny to free himself through
his art—for 'the progress of an artist is a continual self-sacrifice,
a continual extinction of personality'. Of course, the last
formula is no longer Rilke's. It comes from T. S. Eliot's
celebrated declaration of poetry's newly-won independence of
its Romantic past, its return, as Eliot maintained, to an older
tradition;[18] and although Rilke's 'Requiem' is certainly not
'historical', and does not try, like Eliot's essay, to provide a
home for poetry in the house of 'tradition', it yet anticipates by
nine years Eliot's anti-Romantic insurgence.

Rilke in Paris: what is truly important in Rilke's biography
during those years is his learning more and more about his
own art by immersing himself in the art of sculpture and

painting. This had begun at the turn of the century with his stay in the artists' colony in Worpswede near Bremen, where he met two sculptor-painters: Paula Becker, who in 1901 became the wife of the painter Otto Modersohn (and gained fame as Paula Modersohn-Becker), and Clara Westhoff whom he married in the same year. But it was Paris that enriched and deepened his artistic understanding immensely. The measure of this initiation can be gauged by comparing his first lecture-essay on Rodin of 1902, the effusion of an enthusiast, rather vapid and verbose, with the second of 1907, showing a much more disciplined comprehension of the master's work. But the story of his own maturing is written most convincingly into the letters he wrote to Clara about the exhibition of 1907, the *Salon d'Automne* of that year. It was there that Rilke discovered Cézanne; and what he says in these letters about Cézanne amounts to the best possible commentary on his own poetic progress during that period; yet he truly writes about those paintings. '*La réalisation*', he tells Clara, is what Cézanne declared to be the aim of his art;[19] and what he meant was not some vague sense of 'realization', but the 'making real' of the very nature and essence of the object he painted, as if in literal obedience to Schopenhauer's insistence on the Platonic Idea of any given *sujet* being the object of all great art, the Platonic Idea, not the second-hand appearances that our uninitiated senses take for the reality of things. This is why, utterly absorbed '*sur le motif*', Cézanne even missed the funeral of his mother.

Inhuman? Most certainly: as inhuman—or superhuman?—as the ability of a man to disregard his hunger and appetite, indeed even his joy in contemplating a beautiful apple, or an ensemble of them, and to paint it *as it truly is*; to say through his paintings not 'Look here! I love this', but simply: 'Here it is', *is*, as the apple exists, not in order to delight the palate or the eye, or to delude the birds to fly close and pick at it, but to reveal its own being, its indestructible form. Or in Goethe's words: '*Ordinary* observation, the proper understanding of mundane things, is the inheritance of common sense; but the *pure* contemplation of the external form together with the inner being is very rare indeed.'[20] To achieve this pure contemplation, it might be necessary, as Rilke puts it in a passage about Van Gogh, 'to give up everything, life above all', to be poor so that the picture can shine with the 'great radiance from within' that may be the reward of chosen poverty.[21] And Cézanne's obsession, given in to again and again, with the mountain of Sainte Victoire, is in truth the never-satisfied passion to penetrate to the very heart of something that to others is not more than a moderately 'picturesque' piece of landscape. 'The good conscience of those reds, of those blues, their simple truthfulness!', Rilke exclaims, and believes that no one has ever risen in art so far even above love—or dislike or, for that matter, any personal emotion—than Cézanne in his old age: he no longer *judges*, but merely *says*.[22]

It is a mere accident of Rilke's life that he learned from Cézanne what Rembrandt might have taught him with even greater momentum; or what, like Proust, he might have discovered in Vermeer: that art is only the search for a reality undistorted by the self's whims, caprices, or even passions—at least in an epoch which, all but entirely lacking any idea of a transcendental self, knows only selves that seem to consist entirely of whims, caprices and passions. And indeed Rilke himself recognized that the Venetian painters in the Louvre, that Chardin, in whom he saw Cézanne's ancestor, had prepared him for the revelation of the *Salon d'Automne*.[23] And when Fräulein Vollmoeller, his good guide through the exhibition, said of Cézanne that he used to sit in front of his object 'like a dog and simply looked, without any nervousness or ulterior motive'; or when she pointed to the finished parts of a Cézanne-painted apple, saying 'this he knew', and then accounted for the empty part of the same apple by remarking: 'And this he didn't yet know; he painted only what he knew', Rilke exclaimed, 'What a good conscience he must have had!' (as good a conscience, presumably, as his red and blue)[24] and was at that moment filled with the one desire: to attain the same integrity (some of his 'thing-poems', written at that time, possess it) and to conquer within himself all that was still left of his neo-Romantic disposition. He seemed to be bent upon disproving Clara's *bon mot* when, looking into that well in the Certosa of Naples and unable to disentangle what there was in it from the water's reflection of their own faces, she remarked that it was impossible in life to see anything 'without ourselves getting into the picture'. It was Cézanne who, after Rodin, strengthened his resolution to overcome the predicament. Not to get himself into the picture—this is now the dominant ambition of the poet. His letters about Cézanne and Cézanne's 'boundless objectivity', were his reply to Clara's 'subjective' Neapolitan observation.

What is it, we may well ask, that now lends the accent of violence—'*Gewalttätigkeit*' is the word that Rilke used of this artistic determination—to an 'objective' practice of the arts that appeared to be the most peaceful pursuit with Rembrandt, Vermeer, Goethe, not to mention the classical rhythms in which Schopenhauer's prose speaks about it? Why is it that even nature seems to ignore us and that the wind from the sea, passing us by, only seeks its equals in rock and tree? Is it not because of the sense of non-being, the calamity that separates us from gods, angels, men, beasts and things alike, the unbridgeable distance between us and 'being' that the very first lines of the

First Elegy deplore? Is this not the ground of the suspicion that the faintest admixture of our selves would reduce even our evocation of 'things' to naught and make an irreclaimable desert of the world? Therefore, this apple must not be seen as something sweet and edible; this mountain must not be beheld as a memory of walks in the air fragrant with spring or autumn; and even 'the best', love, must stay outside the work. Who are we to *judge*? 'Saying' is all we may be permitted.[25] A detachment so complete is now required of the artist that nothing in his work must suggest that he is delighted with what is delightful, repulsed by what is repugnant, or nauseated by what is nauseating. A century and a half of aesthetic self-consciousness and a great deal of 'history' have sufficed to make what after all is only a new variation on 'negative capability' sound so harsh and so extreme that Keats, its first author, would hardly have recognized it.[26]

'Do you remember', Malte Laurids Brigge writes in a fictitious letter, 'do you remember Baudelaire's incredible poem *Une Charogne* ['Carrion']? Perhaps I understand it now. . . . He was in the right. It was his task to see in this terrible thing, seeming to be only repulsive, the validity of something that, together with all the rest of being, *is*. There is no choice or refusal.'[27] If life is to be affirmed, as Rilke, after all these lessons, seemed to affirm it twenty-five years later in the Ninth Elegy, its horrors would have to be accepted too. Rilke has included passages from his real letters in *Malte Laurids Brigge*, (or passages from the novel in his letters) and among them is a letter to Clara in which he insists upon precisely this, referring even to Flaubert's retelling the legend of Saint-Julien-l'Hospitalier bedding down with a leper and warming him with the warmth of his body. 'You can imagine', he writes to her, 'how it moves me to read that Cézanne in his last years still knew this very poem—Baudelaire's *Charogne*—by heart and used to recite it word for word.' And then Rilke proclaims that he suddenly comprehends the destiny of Malte Laurids Brigge and knows what this book of slow gestation, this *La Nausée* of 1910, will show once it is finished: the truth of Cézanne's insight together with the weakness of Malte, 'for whom it was too tremendous' to live by it as a poet.[28]

Too tremendous? Or too inhuman, too violent? Of course, neither Rilke's words about Cézanne nor Cézanne's words about himself should be taken too literally. They both shared the artist's ambition not to leave anything in a state of vagueness—an ambition named by Rilke in *Malte Laurids Brigge*: 'He was a poet and hated the imprecise' (but certainly not always achieved by himself when he wrote prose), and in pursuing the goal of precision with such singlemindedness, he often came close to being overprecise. Such renunciation of the self as he demanded, such *'réalisations'* as he desired, such 'reifications' as he sought, are impossible. Indeed, might not this red or indeed that blue, in the process of becoming truer and truer and ever more *not* meant to please the human eye, acquire some chill together with the 'good conscience'? It was in the same year—1907—as his momentous discovery of Cézanne, that Rilke could not help speaking of 'violence' even when he intended nothing but praise for Rodin.[29] Surely, he meant the grandly 'violent', 'baroque-expressionist' gestures of the great artist, creator of the Balzac who, from the unlikely starting-point of the *fin de siècle*, seems to stride straight into eternity. Yes, there was violence; and this, Rilke suggests, may explain the resistance with which Rodin's work met in his own time (and, be it added, the—not always respectful—indifference of posterity). And concerning that violence, Rilke attributes it once again to the tragic situation of art in this epoch: that insofar as the artist wanted to remain faithful to what Rilke in the Seventh Elegy calls '*die noch erkannte Gestalt*'—the forms of life still left intact, undistorted, recognizable—he had to seek, 'impatiently, desperately', a concrete equivalent, an 'objective correlative', to *his* inner vision; and this was the more difficult as his vision was left without support or acclaim by what Rilke, in the same essay, called the vague and formless soul of an age that had become intangible, dissolved as it was in an incessant flow, without a face that would outwardly show the *Innenwelt*, the world within.[30]

It is astonishing that he should speak of violence at the same time as speaking of Rodin whom, years before he discovered Cézanne, he admiringly chose as his teacher in self-less objectivity. But the suspicion of force, only marginally hinted at in 1907, was to win out before too long. In the early summer of 1914, still in Paris, only two months before the war would shut him out of this accursed paradise, he proclaimed outright that what he had taken for objectivity in the 'thing-poems' was in truth the forcible invasion of '*die Dinge*', the 'things', by his imagination, or else his making prisoners of them—prisoners of the war between within and without—by enclosing them, despite all the selfless gazing, within the confines of his subjectivity. And if even 'the best', even love, had to be kept out of the artist's conquests, then it became clear to him now that there was a limit to his loveless contemplation of things; for now, after having been seen and observed with such intensity, 'the things' desired to prosper in the artist's love:

> *Denn des Anschauns, siehe, ist eine Grenze.*
> *Und die geschautere Welt*
> *will in der Liebe gedeihen.*

This is the meaning of the turning point announced by the

poem '*Wendung*'. It ends with the poet's recognition that everything has been done that his art can achieve by seeing, watching, gazing, observing: '*Werk des Gesichts ist getan*'; what must begin now is '*Herzwerk*', work of heart. This is how Rilke now, in 1914, interprets the overwhelming message that had come to him two years earlier in the castle of Duino, a message of which later he would speak as solemnly as St John might have talked of the divine text he received on Patmos, a text so urgent that he needed both his hands to write it down. But for the time being, for the ten years between Duino and Muzot, Rilke did not quite understand what the voice that was in the storm demanded of him, the voice that then at last did speak to *him*, not only to the primeval rock. It was in Muzot that it declared itself unmistakably. But Muzot comes after the First World War, after Paris. What in 1914 was felt to be a turning point, the beginning of a movement away from the negation of the human self for the sake of 'things', ended in 1922 in the profoundest possible reversal. Art was no longer 'even beyond love'. On the contrary, love was now called upon to garner things, doomed to be consumed in the ever more voracious meaninglessness of the outside world, into the purified subjectivity within:

> *Nirgends, Geliebte, wird Welt sein, als innen . . .*

'Nowhere can world exist but within . . .' For what is without, loses more and ever more the integrity of its substance. Between 1914 and 1922 there were moments when Rilke, as so many other men of some genius, believed that 'spirit', after its apparently endless withdrawal from external reality, would decide to return. 'A god at last!' Rilke cried in August 1914— and the god was the god of war; and the poet deemed himself happy that after all the years of grey indifference he saw men who were divinely inspired. But it was not only war, it was almost every occasion showing an increase in the temperature of the mind that evoked some enthusiasm in him, whether it was the socialist revolutionary agitation in 1918 Munich, where he lived at the time, or Mussolini's grandiose posturing in Italy. None of these elations lasted—as little as they signalled the Hegelian World Spirit's decision to seek a home for itself on earth rather than in the invisibility of human inwardness. Neither the god of war nor any other illusionist would supply the spirit's present reality to the monuments of the past that still stand among men, beautiful, visited by crowds of spectators and yet hollowed, deserted and endangered: pillars, pylons, the Sphinx, the Cathedral of Chartres, all waiting for their invisible resurrection in us:

> . . . Earth! invisible!
> What is your urgent command, if not this transformation? . . .
> (Ninth Elegy)

First came the poetic glorification of the outside world, the 'things', through the sacrifice of the self, the self's infinite contraction into pure vision, and then followed the amazing *volte-face* of the external world's rejecting such dedication, and desiring, on the contrary, to be transformed into the invisible substance of inwardness. Are these more than the extreme and radically opposed utopias of an artist who, because of his historical situation, is the more intensely an artist the less art knows what to do with itself? It would be easier to let eccentricities be eccentricities were it not for the persistent suspicion that this is more than the story of an artist and his art in a certain age. It reveals with that pointedness and concentration of which only art is capable the vexed relationship, made ever more vexatious in this epoch, between the human self and the world that it inhabits. Ever since Hegel and Marx, this has been called alienation, a painful estrangement that is bound for ever to seek solutions. Marx believed that the 'alienated' human selves can only recover their true humanity by collectively conspiring to change the offending external circumstances. But in Rilke's Parisian poetry the unending attrition of human sensibility, caused by the deadly machinery of the age, is countered by the poetic self's withdrawing from the uneven combat with the world, a withdrawal that T. S. Eliot went so far as to call 'extinction of personality'. Finally, at Muzot, the self has changed its mind. Now it has resolved to assimilate the more and more unpoetic and soulless outside world to man's deepest, truest, and most hidden condition: the condition of the invisible soul. In all its apparent esoteric seclusion Rilke's poetry enacts a metropolitan scene—Paris, the infinite scene—from the modern history of the world.

IV

Thomas Mann in Venice

The autobiographical elements in *Death in Venice* are so obvious
that they would hardly be worth discussing for their own sake;[1]
yet to attend to them means at the same time to contemplate
something that is of greater interest than they are in themselves,
namely, Thomas Mann's art of writing and thus some aspects
of the art of writing as such. It is pleasurable as well as illumin-
ating to watch Thomas Mann as he transforms 'life', his life,
into what Nietzsche called an 'aesthetic phenomenon', a
sensible composition in which every fragment falls into its
seemingly preordained place, thus redeeming what as merely
'lived' experience may appear to be accidental and fragmentary.
This he does by what sometimes looks like (but never is) a mere
record of the experience itself, entrusting its artistic metamorphosis to the recorder's tone of voice, its rhythms, inflex-
ions and cadences: in brief, his style. Then again he merges
what has happened in his own life with occurrences in other
lives, related to his by real similarity or else chosen by him as
'mythological' models, lives upon which myth or history has
already bestowed representative or symbolic stature so that the
reader may experience, with regard to the author, what
Thomas Mann's Lotte, in his Goethe novel *Lotte in Weimar*,
feels when she meets Goethe again—forty-four years after their
notorious Werther time: 'She recognized and yet did not
recognize him.'[2] However, this 'mythologizing' soon begins to
modify the original experience of the artist by colouring it
with the tints of art, so that in the end we are no longer quite
sure how much had to be 'transformed'.

Was what the artist experienced in 'life' perhaps already 'art'? Goethe, I have already observed, once wrote to Frau von Stein (1777): 'You know how symbolic my existence is . . . '; and exactly this kind of artistic sensibility Thomas Mann parodied one-and-a-half centuries later by letting his confidence trickster Felix Krull boast that despite his having fraudulently evaded military service in the most amusing manner, he yet had led a life as disciplined as that of a soldier. 'Although I conducted my life *like* a soldier', the rogue confesses, 'I would yet have to be a country bumpkin if I were to believe that therefore I ought to have been a soldier. Indeed, if I were asked rationally to elaborate and define a preciously indefinable possession of the soul, I would say that freedom resides in the right to live metaphorically, not literally, to live symbolically: *like* a soldier, but not *as* a soldier.'[3] (Kierkegaard, we remember, once said of Goethe in the disapproving tones of the radical moralist that 'as soon as any situation became threatening to him in *life*, he escaped from it by turning it into poetry'. Yet to remove oneself, even in this manner, from the scene of 'the real', means, Kierkgaard said, to 'falsify the ethical nature of human reality'.[4] This is precisely why Thomas Mann's last metaphor of the artist is the confidence-trickster.)

No doubt, a writer like Thomas Mann, or Proust, or Joyce, comes to experience a great deal of what for other people would simply be 'life', as, from the outset, *aesthetic* experience, as representative, quasi-mythological, or symbolic, in short as 'literature'. Franz Kafka once rejected with indignant irony a graphologist's finding that he had 'literary interests'. 'No,' Kafka exclaimed, 'I have no literary interests; I *am* literature!'[5] This might profitably be remembered whenever the discussion of Thomas Mann's works—and of much else in modern literature—reaches the inevitable point at which

THOMAS MANN IN VENICE 75

Life and Art come into view as eternally inimical opposites.

'I *am* literature'—it may well be a little Kafkaesque that Thomas Mann, who like so many artists of his time was plagued by the irreconcilable feud between Art and Life, could say of *Death in Venice*—I am referring to the autobiographical lectures he delivered at Princeton in 1940—that this novella is 'the morally and artistically most pointed and condensed version of the problem of art and decadence'—a problem which could not exist if nobody had ever felt that art and the 'stupid vitality of the ordinary and normal' (as opposed to the refinements of decadence) might be enemies—and yet say *at the same time* that not one of the story's features and incidents had to be invented because everything in it was offered to him 'by reality': 'the suspect gondolier, the boy Tadzio and his family' (the boy, by the way, who a few years ago, with his appearance changed by time into that of an elderly ex-aristocrat in Warsaw, revealed—not implausibly—his once so beautiful identity)— the boy Tadzio, then, and further 'the planned departure frustrated by the luggage mishap, the cholera, the honest-to-goodness clerk in the travel office, the malignant street-singer'.[6]

Death in Venice tells the story of Gustav von Aschenbach, a writer, and thus the autobiographical element becomes all but unavoidable. And it would certainly be surprising—after the blatantly autobiographical *Tonio Kröger*, Thomas Mann's 'portrait of the artist as a young man'—if the points of identity between author and hero were limited to their vocation, or, for that matter, to the initial 'L' of their birthplaces. The second chapter of *Death in Venice* is entirely devoted to Aschenbach's biography, to his life as a writer: for he has had no other life—a fact which is the necessary condition for the tale told. Right at the beginning of this biographical second chapter, it becomes clear that Thomas Mann allowed his fictional author to become famous through works that he, Thomas Mann, had either written himself or intended to produce at one time or another, vicariously completing them instead through Aschenbach.

In fact, we learn nothing of Aschenbach's writings that does not confirm the literary identity of Gustav von Aschenbach and Thomas Mann. The heroes of Aschenbach's fictional world are Thomas Mann's own heroes: those 'moralists of accomplishment' who, always a little like his Frederick of Prussia, are 'modern' heroes by virtue of their almost abstractly moral wills driving them on to achievements the 'meaning' of which they regard with the same scepticism as 'the meaning of life' itself.[7]

The urge surreptitiously to lift the pseudonym and confess his identity with some of his heroes sometimes assumes the form of a mystifying playfulness which Thomas Mann indulged so generously that it is likely to stir into action ever bigger swarms of literary detectives for years to come. In that biographical second chapter of *Death in Venice*, he speaks for instance of Aschenbach's belief, treated again and again in his own fiction, that 'nearly everything great which comes into being does so in spite of something—in spite of sorrow or suffering, poverty, destitution, physical weakness, depravity, passion, or a thousand other handicaps';[8] a conviction which it is said Aschenbach expressed once directly in an inconspicuous place. Certainly we are familiar with this theme, if not through Thomas Mann's Schiller story '*Schwere Stunde*', then through Nietzsche or even Sigmund Freud. But why is there any mentioning of the fact that Aschenbach said so in an inconspicuous place? Because he, Thomas Mann himself, had used these very words, six years before he gave them to Aschenbach, in answering a question about alchohol as a creative stimulant that a rather 'inconspicuous' journal had put to a number of artists.[9]

Yet while such asides proclaim, or perhaps whisper, 'It is I', the revelation may be withdrawn again as if it had been made at a moment of excessive intimacy, or else to ward off the misunderstanding that the 'I' of a work of art could truly be the same as the 'I' of the real person. No, 'art is a heightened mode of existence'. Thomas Mann says this in *Death in Venice* right at the end of the chapter that so intriguingly blends fictional biography with real autobiography; and so, with a determined gesture, he breaks off the autobiographical line he had just drawn. It is as if he wished to say: Of course, this story may never have been told had its author, in his 'real' life, not had certain experiences; but it would be folly to assume that in his writing he simply reports them. The 'I' of literature does not belong to the domain of 'reality'; it is a citizen of the realm of art. Therefore, having unmistakably pointed to the sameness of the real and the fictional author, of Thomas Mann and Gustav von Aschenbach, he now describes the face of Aschenbach after the image of an artist—yes, the image: Thomas Mann clipped it from a newspaper that published the photograph together with the news of the artist's death—an artist very different from himself in appearance and work; and he does so with such realistic suggestiveness that a lithograph, made about ten years later by an illustrator of *Death in Venice*, shows Aschenbach's head as strikingly resembling—Gustav Mahler.[10]

'When I first saw it, I was almost terrified', wrote Thomas Mann in 1921.[11] Why Gustav Mahler? The answer, paradoxically, gives yet another touch of autobiography to what may have been designed to stress the universal meaning of the story by distracting from its autobiographical nature. For at about the time he conceived the story, in the spring of 1911, Thomas

Mann heard of the composer's death; only shortly before, he had made Mahler's acquaintance in Munich and was deeply impressed by his 'self-consuming intensity'. Now the sad news 'mingled with the impressions and ideas that brought forth the story'.[12] This was the reason why he gave to his hero, who would die in a state of ecstatic abandon, not only the first name of the composer, but his features as well, feeling sure that his readers, unaware of the creative coincidence, would never recognize the likeness, and certainly without the slightest premonition that sixty years later a maker of films would transform his Aschenbach into a kind of Gustav Mahler; metamorphosize the classically austere writer and 'conqueror of the abyss',[13] as Aschenbach is called in the story, into a composer who expressed in his music the luxuriant passions of 'the abyss'; replace a determined worshipper of Apollo by an artist who has set to music Nietzsche's song of Dionysus—and would thus undo the tragic irony of Thomas Mann's story: that a determinedly Apollonian writer dies in the embrace of Dionysus, the wild deity of chaos, abandon, and intoxication.

Death in Venice was written between the summers of 1911 and 1912, and was first published by *Die Neue Rundschau* in the autumn of 1912. We shall probably never know for certain what the impressions were that 'brought forth' the story. Yet again it is fascinating and instructive to observe the autobiographical hide-and-seek that Thomas Mann is so fond of playing in the unreliable border-region between the empirical and the imaginative truth.

Thomas Mann's Tonio Kröger, we remember, bitterly complained that emotional aloofness, indeed coldness, on the part of the writer, was a necessary condition of his successfully rendering in literature the life of the passions. This was in fact the theme of *Tonio Kröger*. To dedicate oneself to writing is to freeze one's own feelings; it follows therefore that the poem that formed itself in Tonio's mind during a nocturnal sea voyage when 'his heart was alive' was bad and useless; and it was bad and useless *because* he 'felt'.[14] *Death in Venice*, in turn, is the story of an artist's frozen feelings destructively released by a sudden thaw that makes them flood the soul and annihilate the person.

A little scene in the third chapter of *Death in Venice* supports the Tonio 'dogma'. Aschenbach, having just arrived in his Lido hotel after a somewhat ominous crossing from another Adriatic resort, sets eyes for the first time on the Polish boy Tadzio, and sees with surprise that he possesses that perfect beauty which recalls 'Greek sculpture of the noblest period'.[15] During the lengthy dinner that evening, sitting alone and at some distance from the Polish family, Aschenbach now entertains himself with speculations about beauty, form, and art, only to discover at the end that 'his thoughts ... were like the seemingly felicitous promptings of a dream which, when the mind is sobered, are seen to be completely empty'.[16] Like Tonio Kröger on that ship, his emotions, stirred by Tadzio's beauty, are now alive, and his literary thoughts are therefore without value. Thomas Mann may even have been suggesting the measure of Aschenbach's emotional state by mentioning the feebleness, at that point, of his aesthetic findings.

Yet as if afterwards to disprove the Tonio Kröger 'doctrine', Thomas Mann shows in the fourth chapter how Aschenbach, at the height of his passion for Tadzio, is suddenly seized by a desire to write, and how he does so on the beach and in the sight of Tadzio, deriving from the boy's beauty both his inspiration and his criterion of artistic perfection. Emotional detachment no longer seems to count as the sole condition of good writing; on the contrary, it is, we are told, a short piece of exquisite prose that Aschenbach produces by thus communing with his beloved. After all, as we have seen, Goethe wrote one of his greatest poems, the Marienbad 'Elegy', immediately upon his parting with Ulrike von Levetzow, and called it (to Eckermann, 16 November 1823) 'the product of a greatly impassioned condition'. The greatest happiness of a writer lies now, or so we read in *Death in Venice*, in thoughts that may wholly be transformed into feelings, in feelings that may wholly enter into thoughts. Passion and intellectual articulation are at one.[17]

It is a strange accident of literary history that T. S. Eliot, in the essay on 'Tradition and the Individual Talent' that he wrote in 1917, about fifteen years after *Tonio Kröger* and without knowing the story, joined that 'fictional' German writer in his insistence upon the antithetical relationship between personal emotion and artistic accomplishment,[18] while in 1921, about ten years after *Death in Venice*, he echoed, in his essay on 'The Metaphysical Poets', Thomas Mann's contrary idea by postulating that poets should 'feel their thought as immediately as the colour of a rose'.[19]

Was Thomas Mann himself on the Lido at the time *Death in Venice* began to take shape? He was, in the spring of 1911; and had come there, like Aschenbach, only after he had tried out another seaside resort, Brioni (where he received the news of Gustav Mahler's death).[20] Was there a boy called 'Tadzio'? Very likely; for not only did Thomas Mann himself say that he did not invent the figure; there is also a letter, found among his correspondence, written to him by a Polish lady explaining, undoubtedly at Mann's request, the derivation of the pet name 'Tadzio' that he had first perceived only as a strange sound.[21] Did he write on the Lido a short piece of prose? He did, and the description he gives in *Death in Venice* of Aschenbach's little essay fits his own to a remarkable degree. Aschenbach had been invited to write something personal about a certain 'cultural phenomenon'. He was familiar with the subject in question and it meant much to him. All of a sudden, he felt the irresistible desire to write about it in Tadzio's presence and to let the theme shine with the notorious brilliance of his style.[22] Thomas Mann's own brief essay, written in response to a journal's demand, was 'About the Art of Richard Wagner', dated 'Lido-Venice, May 1911'.[23] The manuscript, now in the Thomas Mann Archive in Zürich, was partly written on paper bearing the letterhead 'Grand Hotel des Bains, Lido-Venise'. Venice and Wagner: *Tristan und Isolde* was partly composed in Venice, above all Isolde's love-death, and it was in Venice that Wagner died.

But the affinity of Thomas Mann's short essay and *Death in Venice* is of a still more intimate nature. The essay tells us that its author's love for Richard Wagner has always been a love without faith: he has never quite trusted the moral integrity of the enchantment. Yet this lack of faith has not diminished his love: 'To me it has always seemed pedantic not to be able to love without belief.' Mann then tries to define his relationship to the composer, and the definition gradually turns to lyrical invocation: 'sceptical', he first calls this relationship, 'pessimistic, clairvoyant, almost resentful'; 'almost resentful'—one remembers, coming upon this, Aschenbach's encounter with Tadzio in the hotel lift when the lover concludes from the condition of Tadzio's teeth (they strike him, as he observes the boy at such close quarters, as weak and slightly defective) that he will not live long; and as Aschenbach thinks this, he is overcome by a feeling of vindication and satisfaction.[24] Almost resentful, then, was Thomas Mann's relationship to Richard Wagner. Just *how* resentful is shown by a letter he wrote at the very time he composed *Death in Venice* and shortly after he had published that essay on Wagner. The essay, he says in the letter, fails in conveying the depth of the crisis he was experiencing in his attitude to Wagner. To test it, he had been to a performance of *Götterdämmerung* and his revulsion from these 'horrendous histrionic displays of tragic passions' expressed itself even as murmured protests.[25] Still, according to the essay his relationship to Wagner is not only 'almost resentful, but passionate throughout, an indescribable seduction to live'. And instantly the essay becomes hymnical:

Wonderful hours of profound happiness, enjoyed in solitude among crowds in the theatre, hours tremulous with shocks of bliss, full of delight for nerves and mind, and of insights into things of touching and great significance as only this insurpassable art can yield.

Is this the way one speaks of a musical-theatrical experience? Or, rather, of sensations provided by Eros? 'Touching and great'—this deliberately incongruous combination of adjectives Thomas Mann used again, on another occasion that would have some bearing on *Death in Venice*. In a letter he wrote in the summer of 1920 to a critic by the name of Weber,[26] who was at the time a teacher in the free educational community of Wickersdorf, he calls 'touching and great' the story of Goethe's falling in love, at the age of 74, with a girl of 19, the story that Mann, under the title of 'Goethe in Marienbad', planned to write in 1911 and which, as he himself said in another letter, 'became *Death in Venice*'. But concerning the Wagnerian hours spent in the theatre: put the beach in the place of the theatre, and beauty in the place of art, and those sentences written by Mann on notepaper of a Lido hotel exactly describe the hours Aschenbach spent by the sea, passionately observing Tadzio, who, silhouetted against the infinity of sky and water, merged at the end with stirring, great, and significant memories of the myth of Hermes, the beautiful guide of the dead (a god that afterwards acquired a kind of omnipresence in the writings of Thomas Mann).

There is, however, not merely an emotional connection between Mann's essay on Wagner and *Death in Venice*; their intellectual vicinity is equally close. For Mann's love of Wagner's art was not only sceptical, not only 'almost resentful' and passionate; it also lacked belief—belief, above all, in the future of that art. Wagner, he wrote, was 'through and through nineteenth-century', indeed he was 'the representative German artist of an epoch' that will be remembered 'perhaps as great and certainly as unhappy and unfortunate'. When Mann tried to imagine what the masterpiece of the twentieth century would be like, he imagined something essentially different from Wagner's works, and 'differing from them, as I believe, to its advantage'. Such a masterpiece would be, he hoped, distinguished by its logic, form, and clarity; would be austere and yet serene; more detached, nobler and healthier than Wagner's operas: 'something that seeks greatness not in the colossal and the baroque, and beauty not in the ecstatic'.[27] Unmistakably, it is Aschenbach's aesthetic ideal that Thomas Mann adumbrates in criticizing Wagner: Aschenbach's renunciation of the 'abyss', of the inebriation of Dionysus, of the moral laxity inherent in all 'psychological' understanding ('*Tout comprendre, c'est tout pardonner*'), and his single-minded dedication instead to a new simplicity and harmony of form which 'henceforth was to give his productions such a deliberate stamp of mastery and classicism'.[28] This, then, is said in *Death in Venice* of Gustav von Aschenbach; and the passage from Thomas Mann's essay on Wagner ends with the prognostication: 'A new classicism, it seems to me, is bound to come.' There can be no doubt left: *Death in Venice*, like *Tonio Kröger*, is a highly autobiographical tale, reflecting important developments in Thomas Mann's emotional *and* intellectual life (and, as one likes to add after seeing the film, changes also in his artistic sensibility which indeed is very different from that of Gustav Mahler).

'A new classicism': this marks the point at which the relations between the belief Thomas Mann has *expressed* in the essay as his own, and the belief he has *embodied* in the story, become most confusing and problematical. He may well have intended to write a 'classical' work. But is *Death in Venice* an example, or even a promise and token, of such a conquest of the 'abyss', such a recovery of classical simplicity, or such a 'miracle of regained innocence' as, according to the 'biography', came about in Aschenbach's art after he had left behind all those complexities of knowledge and understanding that inhibit or frustrate the classical moral resolve?[29] Far from it. Mann himself seemed not a little baffled by the discrepancy between intention and result. It may be true to say—and he who says it can draw support not only from the essay on Wagner but also from the letter to Weber—that he tried to adopt in all seriousness Aschenbach's classicistic diction. For even in the letter written almost a decade after the 'classical' critique of Wagner and the publication, too, of *Death in Venice*, he says that it was his aim to achieve that balance between the sensual and the moral that Goethe had ideally accomplished in *Elective Affinities*, a novel which Thomas Mann remembers having read five times while writing his story.[30] Is it likely that he did so only to learn the secret of the mature Goethe's prose style? No, the theme also of *Elective Affinities* must have been of the greatest interest to him: the tragic derangements caused by erotic passion, and the opposition between 'civilization' and passionate 'discontent', between the 'garden' and the wilderness of nature. For this is precisely the clash that is also at the centre of

Death in Venice. Its every scene is vibrant with the shocks of the war between order and jungle, divine beauty and Indian cholera, serenity of mind and consuming passion, clear articulation and enticingly wild sounds of the 'Panic' flute.

To use a mythological shortcut: both *Elective Affinities* and *Death in Venice* tell of the conflict between Apollo and Dionysus; and it was Nietzsche, one of the young Thomas Mann's educators, who made this tension between the 'Apollonian' and the 'Dionysian' the central theme of his celebrated book on the origins of Greek tragedy. Apollo and Dionysus: both Goethe's *Elective Affinities* and Thomas Mann's *Death in Venice* prove that these two deities knew how to survive their dethronement by a mythless age; and it is a revealing coincidence of literary history that about the same time as Thomas Mann's writing *Death in Venice*, Rilke began the third of his *Duino Elegies* which moves entirely in the field of tension between garden and jungle, while Dr Freud opened, as it were, his psychoanalytical practice with the distinction between *Ego* and *Id*, the 'I' and the 'It', the conscious and the unconscious, without, alas, preventing Europe from losing herself a few years later in the machine jungle of the war.

Certainly, the experience that occasioned the story *Death in Venice* must have been passionate enough; Mann in his letter to Weber calls the inspiration for his story 'hymnic', but continues by saying that his own artistic nature forced him to 'objectify' the experience and thus to detach himself from it. Indeed, one may conclude that Mann himself at that time was assailed by the 'Dionysian' spirit, a spirit 'socially irresponsible in its subjective lyricism'; that 'extraordinary emotions', intoxicating and overpowering, seized hold of his soul; and that this soul tried to express itself 'hymnically'. Yet, disciplined by artistic restraint and ethical discrimination, he wrote 'a moral fable'.[31] Goethe once expressed himself in a similar manner about *Elective Affinities* when he thought that he had to defend his work against the charge of immorality;[32] and Thomas Mann wrote of *Death in Venice*, when he first mentioned the subject in the summer of 1911, that it was, despite its apparent moral dubiousness, a 'very proper' story.[33]

The artistic preponderance of the Apollonian over the Dionysian, a new classicism, objectivity, restraint, the 'ideal balance', such as Goethe had accomplished in his 'moral fable' *Elective Affinities*, were affirmed by Thomas Mann; and this bears witness to his serious 'classical' intentions. Yet the witness is unreliable. About a year before he had written that 'classical' letter, he had written another in which he said: 'Between you and me, the style of my story is somewhat *parodistic*. It is a kind of mimicry that I love and spontaneously practise.'[34] And on many occasions after this, Mann disclaimed as his own legitimate property the story's 'hieratic' and classically measured diction, and drew attention instead to its 'parodistic' nature.

Indeed, Thomas Mann employed henceforth, again and again and ever more audaciously, this parodistic method whose secret is a premeditated and aesthetically mastered incongruity between the message delivered and the tone of voice in which it is delivered, between the outrageous tale and the conciliatory bearing of the language that does the telling. The outward literary gesture seems to ask challengingly: 'Who, after this testimony, is prepared to suggest that the classical tradition of literature is seriously disturbed?', while the story, despite its being so decorously narrated, answers most emphatically: 'I.'

Nowhere is this kind of 'parody' more successful than in *Death in Venice*, where content and form are at most skilfully arranged loggerheads. For the composition could not be more classical. It reflects what is *said* of Aschenbach at the beginning: that he classically triumphed over the forces of formlessness and decomposition. Yet what is *shown* through this composition is the utter defeat of a classical campaign so disastrously waged out of season. The irony of this situation, profoundly moral and untouched by mockery, is Thomas Mann's way of acknowledging the tragically simultaneous presence of two incompatible forces within him: a conservative love of the classical literary tradition, and the disruptive insight that, alas, this tradition has had its day. It is once again the love without faith which, as he confessed, determined also his relationship to Wagner. *Death in Venice* conjures up, by means even of an occasional hexameter's intruding into the prose narrative—'*ruhte die Blüte des Hauptes in unvergleichlichem Liebreiz*'—the memory of classical antiquity, but only to set against it the fate of an artist destroyed by the Beautiful in its catastrophic ambivalence: Aschenbach suffers his *Liebestod* by a sea as blue as the Archipelago, but dies in the vicinity of art's own city that has been ravished by the Asiatic plague (which, by the way, has got to Italy along the same route that once upon a time the god from the East, from Asia, Dionysus, travelled to Greece—according to Nietzsche's disputed tracing of his path).

It was Thomas Mann's love for the music of Richard Wagner that made him translate the musical device of the *leitmotif*, so characteristic of Wagner's operatic compositions, into the language of literature, using it with ever greater subtlety in his novels and stories. In his first novel, *Buddenbrooks*, it is employed with epic simplicity, either in the Homeric form of the *epitheton ornans*, a characteristic of a person's appearance or manner that is repeated whenever the person is mentioned, or in the form of identical phrases that help the reader to recognize a significant similarity of recurring events or situations. In *Death in*

Venice the *leitmotif* has both these functions to which, however, is added the ironical and weightier task of giving the highest degree of compositional order to this story of increasing disorder and decomposition. Like verse and rhyme in poetry, *leitmotif* speaks the language of form, and therefore of art, even when the speech itself says: form and art are done for.

If Thomas Mann had written, instead of *Death in Venice*, the work he first intended to write, the story of Goethe in Marienbad, 'this painful, touching and great story which one day I may write after all', as he put it in the letter to Weber, its theme would also have been, according to this and several other published letters, the fate of an artist overpowered by an 'impossible' passion, a passion capable of afflicting soul and mind with feverish ecstasies, and the person with grievous and even grotesque humiliations. The story would have been of the old Goethe at the height of his fame, a European legend of poetry and wisdom, sage of '*Entsagung*', of resignation and 'classical' restraint, now passionately, and therefore desperately, in love with a girl of 19 and in all earnestness proposing to marry her. It is obvious how much 'Goethe in Marienbad' would have had in common with *Death in Venice*. Thomas Mann might even have exploited the subject's grotesque and humiliating possibilities beyond the limits of recorded biography and even to the point of perverting the biographical: for instance, 'Mama', the girl's 'ambitious and procuring' mother, might, as Mann's letter to Weber suggests, have done her best to bring about the scandalous match. But in the end the young Ulrike von Levetzow proved not quite right as the amorous occasion for utterly confounding the spirit with absurd promises of happiness and erotic delight. It had to be the boy Tadzio.

Why? Thomas Mann's letter to Weber tries to explain how he came to abandon the plan of 'Goethe in Marienbad' and decided to write *Death in Venice* instead. Yet he could not quite help hinting here and there in the Venetian story at the neighbourly relations between the poet in Marienbad and the writer in Venice. It would, for instance, be surprising if the two wax candles that, as the second chapter tells us, Aschenbach was in the habit of putting at the head of his manuscript,[35] had nothing to do with the two wax candles that, according to Eckermann's *Conversations with Goethe*, were ceremoniously placed at Goethe's desk when Eckermann was first allowed to see the manuscript of the Marienbad 'Elegy';[36] or if the letter Goethe wrote to Zelter about the tremendous effect music had upon him during that Marienbad summer—it 'unfolded' his soul as 'amicably one opens and flattens a clenched fist'[37]—were not responsible for the characterization of Aschenbach by a 'sharp observer': ' "You see, Aschenbach has always lived like this", and the speaker contracted the fingers of his left hand into a fist; "never like this", and he let his open hand drop comfortably from the arm of his chair.'[38]

What made Thomas Mann move his literary stage from Marienbad to Venice was, as he wrote to Weber, 'a private and lyrical travel experience' which persuaded him to 'go to the very limit by introducing the motif of the "forbidden love" '. This explanation, despite its proper reticence, is clear enough; but it can hardly be correct. Considering the extraordinary closeness of the two subjects, it would be surprising indeed if the idea of 'Goethe in Marienbad' had not had its source in the same 'travel experience' as *Death in Venice*. It is much more likely that Thomas Mann first tried to cover the all too autobiographical with the mantle of Goethe, and failed. He all but says so himself in a letter written in September 1915: 'Originally I had planned nothing less than the story of Goethe's last love . . ., a terrible, beautiful, grotesque and deeply stirring tale . . . which became *Death in Venice*. I believe that this "history" of the novella reveals its original intent',[39] namely to show the tragic downfall of a master from the heights of his classical dignity. Well, 'lyrical experiences', while allowing their metamorphosis into literature, have a way of determining after their own will the degrees of revelation and disguise; and the criterion, strange though this may sound in the domain of fiction, is truth.

There is no other writer of his time who has been as conscious as Thomas Mann of the problems besetting the relationship between Life and Art. His work gives the measure of this unceasing preoccupation. From *Buddenbrooks* through *Tonio Kröger* and *Death in Venice* to the novels of his old age, *Doctor Faustus* and, in its comic way, *Felix Krull*, this troublesome pair of opposites was never lost sight of. Whatever may be the 'essential' nature of this relationship, its perplexities have certainly been considerably accentuated by historical accident or, if Hegel was right, by historical necessity. It was certainly not accidental that the link, or perhaps, the gulf, between experience and its articulation, between the material of life and its artistic presentation, between autobiography and the literary work, has for so long attracted so much aesthetic philosophizing. The relation between art and life has become so strained, uncertain and problematical that ever more artists have, in their work, dared the flight into a sphere that is no longer that of life as it is actually lived, and no longer shows or even demands a recognizable connection with the 'concreteness' of human existence. Shunning the ever more difficult alliance with the 'real', art has been tempted to settle where it is at last left to itself: in the sphere of abstraction and pure form. Thomas Mann showed the daring, misery and fatality of this emigration in

Doctor Faustus. His own work as a literary artist was determined by his profound awareness of this historical temptation and at the same time by his moral resolve not to give in to it; for such a resignation would implicitly dismiss life as something utterly unresponsive to the desire for meaning, order, or spiritual perfection, and thus declare it unworthy of the attentions of art.

From this inner awareness springs Thomas Mann's ironical traditionalism, which modelled itself on the classical products of literary history but at the same time could not help 'parodying' them. The author who has so often been hypnotized by the 'abyss' that had opened between reality and art, between the living self and the creative self, has yet in his ironical and 'parodistic' manner succeeded in aesthetically redeeming much real autobiography, that is 'life', through art, through literature. A most exquisite example of this is *Death in Venice*.

NOTES

I. GOETHE IN MARIENBAD

With so many editions of Goethe's works available, I have made reference to chapters of individual works, often within the text itself. Poems are identified by their titles, letters and conversations by their dates as well as the names of the recipients of letters or partners in conversation.

1. Title (*'Liebschaft'*) under which Goethe himself subsumed six short poems addressed to Ulrike von Levetzow in 'Ausgabe letzter Hand' of his works.
2. *Tagebücher 1810–1832*, September 1823 and conversation with Eckermann, 16 November 1823.
3. Conversation with Eckermann, 16 November 1823.
4. To Weygand, 23 March 1824.
5. Zelter's diary note, November 1823.
6. Conversation with Eckermann, 27 October 1823.
7. Police report of 21 July 1823, quoted in Johannes Urzidil, *Goethe in Böhmen*, Zürich and Stuttgart 1962, 159.
8. To Ottilie von Goethe, 3 August 1823 and *Tagebücher*, 14 August 1823.
9. Conversation with Julie von Egloffstein as reported by von Müller, 22 May 1822.
10. *Wilhelm Meisters Lehrjahre*, Book 8, chapter 7.
11. To Ulrike, 10 September 1823.
12. Baron Foelkersahm to his family in Riga, 30 August 1823.
13. To Ottilie von Goethe, 18 August 1823.
14. 25 August 1823.
15. August Sauer, *Ulrike von Levetzow und ihre Erinnerungen an Goethe*, Munich 1904, 11f.
16. *Tagebücher*, 3 September 1823.
17. 'Epochs of the Spirit, based on Hermann's Newest Records', a short review essay of Goethe's first published in 1817 in *Kunst und Altertum*.
18. *Maximen und Reflexionen*, 998 (in the numbering of Max Hecker's edition, Weimar 1907.
19. Schiller's couplet 'Sprache' in the sequence entitled *Votivtafeln*.

20. To Zelter, 26 March 1816.
21. To Zelter, 3 December 1812.
22. To Zelter, 26 March 1816.
23. Nietzsche, *The Birth of Tragedy*, section 5.
24. Kierkegaard, *Stadien auf dem Lebenswege*. (My translation of the German rendering; the corresponding passage, translated by Walter Lowrie, can be found in *Stages of Life's Way*, New York 1967, 152f.).

II. NIETZSCHE IN THE WASTE LAND

References to Nietzsche's works are, in my own translations, to *Gesammelte Werke*, Musarion-Ausgabe, Munich 1920–9 (abbreviated M.A.). With one exception I have not used published translations. This does not imply a judgement on their quality but is simply due to an old habit (quite apart from the fact that some passages from the posthumous writings have never been translated into English). The exception is Walter Kaufmann's translation of *Zarathustra* in *The Portable Nietzsche*, Viking Press, New York 1954 (abbreviated P.N.).

1. M.A. XXI, 251f.
2. M.A. XIII, 25.
   (P.N. 137).
3. Ibid., 25f.
   (P.N. 138).
4. M.A. XV, 13.
5. M.A. IX, 7.
6. M.A. XIII, 166f.
   (P.N. 238f).
7. M.A. XVI, 36f.
8. M.A. III, 5.
9. M.A. XIII, 321.
10. M.A. X, 22.
11. M.A. X, 247.
12. M.A. XIX, 19.
13. M.A. XV, 243f.
14. M.A. XV, 246.
15. M.A. XV, 248.

16. M.A. XII, 253f.
17. M.A. XI, 187.
18. M.A. XIV, 121.
19. M.A. XIV, 187.
20. M.A. XVIII, 45.
21. M.A. XIII, 26.
    (P.N. 138f).
22. M.A. XVIII, 3, 52.
23. M.A. XIII, 26f.
    (P.N. 139).
24. M.A. IV, 183, 310ff.
25. M.A. III, 46.
26. *Schiller's Werke*,
    Insel-Ausgabe IV, 533ff.
27. M.A. XVIII, 356.
28. cf. M.A. XVIII, 62f.
29. M.A. XIII, 166f.
30. M.A. XVIII, 57, 309.
31. M.A. XVII, 249.

III. RILKE IN PARIS

References to Rilke's works are to *Sämtliche Werke*, edited in collaboration with Ruth Sieber-Rilke by Ernst Zinn, Insel-Verlag, Frankfurt a. M. 1957–66 (abbreviated S.W.). Letters are identified by the names of the recipients and the dates, poems (they can be found in many editions of Rilke's poetry) only by their titles.

1. To Countess von Nordeck zu Rabenau.
2. To Countess Manon zu Solms-Laubach, 20 June 1907.
3. To Anton Kippenberg, 25 March 1910.
4. To Princess Marie von Thurn und Taxis-Hohenlohe, 11 February 1922.
5. To Hedwig Fischer, 25 October 1911.
6. S.W. VI, 986.
7. S.W. VI, 709.
8. To Baroness M., 27 October 1920.
9. S.W. VI, 785.
10. T. S. Eliot, *Selected Essays*, London 1948, 145.
11. S.W. VI, 756.
12. S.W. VI, 767.
13. *Das Testament*, Bibliothek Suhrkamp 414, Frankfurt a. M. 1975, 43.
14. S.W. VI, 727.
15. To Lou Andreas-Salomé, 26 June 1914.
16. To Richard Woodhouse, 27 October 1818.
17. To Frau von Stein, 8 March 1808.
18. T. S. Eliot, op. cit., 17.
19. To Clara Rilke, 9 October 1907.
20. Goethe, *Maximen und Reflexionen*, 533 (in the numbering of Max Hecker's edition, Weimar 1907.)
21. To Clara Rilke, 3 October 1907.
22. To Clara Rilke, 13 October 1907.
23. To Clara Rilke, 8 October 1907.
24. To Clara Rilke, 12 October 1907.
25. To Clara Rilke, 13 October 1907.
26. To George and Thomas Keats, 21 December 1817.
27. S.W. VI, 775.
28. To Clara Rilke, 19 October 1907.

29. S.W. v, 241.
30. S.W. v, 240.

IV. THOMAS MANN IN VENICE

References to Thomas Mann's works are to *Stockholmer Gesamtausgabe*, S. Fischer Verlag, Frankfurt a. M. 1945–65 (the volumes are not numbered but have only individual titles). Letters are identified by the names of recipients and by the dates. The quotations—in my own translations—come mostly from the edition of letters made by Erika Mann, 3 volumes, Frankfurt a. M., 1961, 1963, and 1965.

1. For some autobiographical quotations from Notebooks in the Thomas Mann Archive (Zürich) I am indebted to Herbert Lehnert's book *Thomas Mann: Fiktion, Mythos, Religion*, Stuttgart 1965, and to Hans Wysling's article 'Aschenbach's Werke' in the 95th volume of *Euphorion, a Journal for the History of Literature*, Heidelberg 1965, 272ff.

2. *Lotte in Weimar*, 389.

3. *Bekenntnisse des Hochstaplers Felix Krull*, 127.

4. Kierkegaard, see note 24 to 'Goethe in Marienbad'.

5. Letter to Felice, 14 August 1913.

6. Blätter der Thomas Mann-Gesellschaft, Zürich 1966, No. 6, 19, 20.

7. *Ausgewählte Erzählungen*, 466f.

8. Ibid., 465.

9. *Reden und Aufsätze*, II, 678f.

10. *Ausgewählte Erzählungen*, 470f.

11. To Wolfgang Born, 18 March 1921.

12. Ibid.

13. *Ausgewählte Erzählungen*, 468.

14. Ibid., 177.

15. Ibid., 485.

16. Ibid., 488.

17. Ibid., 512.

18. *Selected Essays*, London 1948, 13ff.

19. Ibid., 287.

20. To Hans von Hülsen, 15 June 1911.

21. Cf. Herbert Lehnert, op. cit., 21.

22. *Ausgewählte Erzählungen*, 512f.

23. *Reden und Aufsätze*, II, 693–5.
24. *Ausgewählte Erzählungen*, 497.
25. To Ernst Bertram, 11 August 1912.
26. To Weber, 4 July 1920.
27. *Reden und Aufsätze*, II, 695.
28. *Ausgewählte Erzählungen*, 468.
29. Ibid.
30. To Weber, 4 July 1920.
31. 'Gesang vom Kindchen', quoted in the letter to Weber, 4 July 1920.
32. Conversation with von Rühle (as reported by Varnhagen von Ense in his diary entry of 28 June 1843) and to Joseph Stanislaus Zauper, 7 September 1821.
33. To Philipp Witkop, 18 July 1911.
34. To Josef Ponten, 6 June 1919.
35. *Ausgewählte Erzählungen*, 464.
36. Conversation with Eckermann, 27 October 1823.
37. 24 August 1823.
38. *Ausgewählte Erzählungen*, 463.
39. To Elisabeth Zimmer, 6 September 1915.

INDEX